# MEDICAL CANNABIS

## PATIENT ADVOCATE

**Health**Scouter
WWW.HEALTHSCOUTER.COM

HealthScouter.com - Equity Press
5055 Canyon Crest Drive
Riverside, California 92507

www.healthscouter.com

Purchasing this book entitles you to free updates at medicalcannabisacademy.com

Edited By: Shana McKibbin
Foreword by Lanny Swerdlow, RN

Includes Medical Cannabis from Wikipedia http://en.wikipedia.org/wiki/Medical_cannabis

HealthScouter Medical Marijuana Qualified Patient Advocate: Medical Cannabis Treatment and Medical Uses of Marijuana

ISBN 978-1-60332-119-8

**Important**

NEVER DISREGARD PROFESSIONAL MEDICAL ADVICE, OR DELAY SEEKING IT, BECAUSE OF SOMETHING YOU HAVE READ IN THIS BOOK. ALWAYS SEEK PROFESSIONAL MEDICAL ADVICE BEFORE ACTING UPON INFORMATION READ IN THIS BOOK.

HealthScouter and Equity Press do not provide medical advice. The contents of this book are for informational purposes only and are not intended to substitute for professional medical advice, diagnosis or treatment. Always seek advice from a qualified physician or health care professional about any medical concern, and do not disregard professional medical advice because of anything you may read in this book or on a HealthScouter Web site. The views of individuals quoted in this book are not necessarily those of HealthScouter or Equity Press.

While this book is intended to be a medium for the exchange of information and ideas, it is not meant in any way to be a substitute for sound medical advice; neither should it be viewed as a trusted source of such advice. The views expressed in these messages are not those of any qualified medical association, and the publisher is not responsible for the validity of the information communicated herein or for consequences that may arise from acting upon this information. The publisher is not responsible for any content found in the book that may be deemed offensive, inappropriate, inaccurate or medically unsound. The information you find here is only for the purpose of discussion and should not be the basis for any medical decision. The content is not intended to be a substitute for professional medical advice, diagnosis or treatment.

The information presented is not to be considered complete, nor does it contain all medical resource information that may be relevant, and therefore it is not intended to be a substitute for seeking medical treatment and/or appropriate care.

By reading this book and parts of the Web site, you agree under all circumstances to hold harmless, and to refrain from seeking remedy from, the owners of this book. The publisher shall disclaim all liability to you for damages, costs or expenses, including legal and medical fees, related to your reliance on anything derived from this book or Web site or its contents. Furthermore, Equity Press assumes no liability for any and all claims arising out of the said use, regardless of the cause, effects, or fault.

Equity Press and HealthScouter do not endorse any company or product, and listing on the HealthScouter Web site is not linked to corporate sponsorship. We do not make a claim to being comprehensive or up to date. If you would like to recommend information to include in this book, please contact us – we would be very happy to hear from you.

Purchasing this book entitles you to free updates as they are available. Please register your book at www.healthscouter.com

# *There is a bright future in medical cannabis!*

# TABLE OF CONTENTS

# FOREWORD

*By Lanny Swerdlow, RN*

Cannabis has been used safely and effectively over the known course of human history – from Chinese physicians providing cannabis to patients for pain relief 5,000 years ago to just seventy years ago when your grandparents could go down to the corner drugstore and obtain all kinds of medical preparations of cannabis to treat a veritable cornucopia of ailments such as pain, insomnia, depression, nausea, and drug and alcohol dependence.

Through appeals to racism, greed and avarice, vested interests of people such as newspaper magnate William Randolph Hearst, and the thousands of law enforcement personnel suddenly unemployed at the height of the Great Depression when Prohibition came to an end, conspired to make this ubiquitous plant product found in everybody's medicine cabinet into a drug so horrible and dangerous that even a doctor could not provide it to their patients.

The law they created, the Marijuana Tax Act of 1937, had much to do with industrial competition from hemp for the petrochemical, synthetic fiber and paper industries, and little to do with ingestion of cannabis.

In fact, the AMA testified at the Marijuana Tax Act hearings that they had contacted 10 different federal agencies and not one had any data substantiating the outrageous claims being made by Federal Bureau of Narcotics Director, Harry Anslinger.

Now patients had no choice other than to use the patented prescription drugs manufactured by pharmaceutical corporations. The relief they obtain from these drugs is usually more expensive, more dangerous and, in many cases, less effective than what could be obtained from cannabis.

As cannabis disappeared from the corner drugstore, Americans were denied access to what FDA Chief Administrative Law Judge Francis Young ruled in a 1988 rescheduling hearing as "one of the safest therapeutically active agents known to man...". He recommended rescheduling cannabis so doctors could prescribe cannabis as they had for thousands of years but the Food and Drug Administrator (FDA) Director John Law, a George H.W. Bush appointee, rejected Judge Young's findings and recommendation.

Although all the lay person ever hears about is THC, tetrahydrcannabinol, the psycho-active cannabinoid found in cannabis, there are over 60 other cannabinoids which regulate many of the biological processes that are found in every system in the body.

The cannabinoids found in cannabis interact with your body's cannabinoid system which is involved in regulating a host of biological processes, including pain management, memory formation, sleep, appetite, movement, and even pleasure and emotion.

The cannbinoid system is an intricate component in the biological survival of complex organisms. Over hundreds of millions of years of evolutionary history, as vertebrate animals evolved and became more complex, the cannbinoid system evolved alongside this developing complexity as a means of maintaining homoeostasis, i.e the cannabinoid system maintains the biological balance necessary for healthy life.

Maintaining balance is fundamental to staying healthy. When we are out of balance, we feel sick, as a disease is really nothing more than something that knocks us out of balance. The aging process is essentially our bodies getting more and more out of balance until we are so totally out of balance that we die. Controlling inflammation is essential to maintaining balance and it is by controlling inflammation that cannabis helps maintain our balance.

Inflammation is critical for the maintenance of life – we could not survive without inflammatory processes such as digestion or immunity reactions. Inflammatory processes carry out their function by producing free radicals, but excess free radicals, those produced beyond our need, have been implemented in the aging process as well as in a host of age-related illnesses such as cancer and cardiovascular disease.

By controlling inflammation, by culling it back where it is no longer needed, the cannbinoids in cannabis reduce the formation of free radicals. It is by reducing the formation of free radicals that the cannabinoids found in cannabis can slow the onset of age-related illnesses.

In addition, there has been a virtual cascade of peer-reviewed research studies demonstrating the potent anti-cancer properties of the cannabinoids found in cannabis. In 2003, Dr. Manual Guzman from the University of Madrid authored a medically astounding report detailing current research into the ability of the cannabinoids in cannabis to control the spread of cancer, including the results of his studies on cannabinoids injected into the brains of rats with brain tumors. Published in the peer-reviewed research publication Nature Reviews Cancer, he wrote:

Cannabinoids inhibit tumour growth in laboratory animals. They do so by modulating key cell-signalling pathways, thereby inducing direct growth arrest and death of tumour cells, as well as by inhibiting tumour angiogenesis and metastasis. Cannabinoids are selective antitumour compounds, as they can kill tumour cells without affecting their non-transformed counterparts.

In November 2007, researchers at the California Pacific Medical Center Research Institute published a report showing that the non-psychoactive cannabinoid cannabidiol found in cannabis can inhibit the spread of breast cancer.

Investigators at the University of Wisconsin School of Medicine and Public Health reported in January 2008 that the administration of cannabinoids halts the spread of a wide range of cancers, including brain cancer, prostate cancer, breast cancer, lung cancer, skin cancer, pancreatic cancer, and lymphoma. Like Dr. Guzman's research, the report noted that cannabis offers significant advantages over standard chemotherapy treatments because the cannabinoids in cannabis are both non-toxic and can uniquely target malignant cells while ignoring healthy ones.

Since for the vast majority of people, cannabis has no negative side effects and only beneficial effects, these studies would seem to suggest that the regular appropriate ingestion of cannabis as an agent of cancer prevention would be a prudent course of action.

The cannabinoids are even involved in our emotional responses. Raphael Mechoulam, who discovered of THC, has speculated that cannabinoids are involved in the process by which the brain "translates objective reality into subjective emotions." Essentially if you see someone who makes you feel happy, it is the biochemical mechanism of the cannabinoid system that takes the sight of that person and creates the emotion of happiness.

The cannabinoids produced by your body and those found in cannabis interact with your body's cannabinoid system, which is involved in regulating a host of biological processes including pain management, memory formation, sleep, appetite, movement and even pleasure and emotion. Cannabis, the only plant that thoroughly interacts with our cannbinoid system, provides safe and effective relief from the myriad ailments that wreck havoc with these biological processes.

The elimination of marijuana from our nation's medicine cabinet was one of the major calamities to befall our nation's health care system in the 20th century. Restoring cannabis to its rightful place will be one of the significant achievements of the 21st century, resulting in significant improvement to the health of both the individual and the community.

Far from being detrimental to our community's health, the appropriate use of cannabis increases the health of the community in the same way that the appropriate use of calcium and other supplements do.

Cannabis sets the gold standard for both safety and efficacy, and few other drugs can match it. Rather than discouraging individuals from utilizing cannabis medicinally, our communities would be well served if patients had readily available access to this ancient medicinal herb.

# INTRODUCTION AND MOTIVATION

Dear Reader,

I like to think of myself as a polite, well-reasoned person. I rarely speak out or complain. When a waitress spills something on me, or if my meal is cold—or if I'm overcharged—I generally try to be as polite as possible. I don't like to make very many waves. I often secretly hope that the manager will hear about my predicament and come out and offer me a free meal, or something similar. I generally hope that my polite and respectful demeanor pays off. And it does happen from time to time. You know, I think many people are brought up to believe that this is just good manners. It's how you're supposed to behave. And if you knew me personally, I think you'd agree that I'm generally pretty reserved. Of course my wife may raise an objection or two (!), but I really believe that it's important to treat others as you would like to be treated. We're talking about the golden rule here—it works well and it applies to almost every life circumstance.

But I have to admit that when it comes to my health, or the health of someone I care about—all bets are off. I want to know what's going on—when, why, where, and how. And I make these feelings known. I tend to get downright assertive. It's just something I feel very strongly about. And I feel that when you are in a hospital, or if you're brushing up against the healthcare system, that you should feel the same way. It's unfamiliar turf, and the professionals who work in this system often take advantage of their positions. They may use some jargon to hide the whole truth—or they may say something without checking to make sure you understand completely. They may present the options that are best for them, perhaps the most profitable or convenient. Now I'm not saying this goes on everywhere. There are many professionals in the business of health who go out of their way to make sure you have the best care. And I'm not suggesting that you should become a bully, or purposefully annoying—absolutely not. But I am suggesting that I think it's OK for you to step outside of your typical comfort zone, and put on your patient advocate hat. Because you, the patient or patient advocate, care the most about your care—not the medical system or healthcare providers.

HealthScouter was created to help patients become better advocates for their own medical care. Because when it comes to your healthcare, the stakes are high. There are none higher. And healthcare is one area where consumers (us, the sick people) are notoriously unaware of their options. And that's why I'm publishing these books. To help you understand your options, and to help you get the best care possible. I want to help you become a better advocate for yourself and for your loved ones.

It's my sincere hope that you can take this book with you to the hospital, to be read in the waiting room or by the bedside—and when you see a relevant patient comment you can use this book to ask questions of your health care providers. My advice: Ask lots of questions! Providers are busy people who generally go about their business with little questioning, delivering care as they see fit—making quick decisions—and again, nobody is going to care as much about your health as you. So now, more than ever, you need tools at your disposal to get the best care possible. One of the tools at your disposal is this HealthScouter book and the material within. You need to be armed with questions, and you need to ask questions all of the time. And so the difficult part is now to understand the right questions to ask.

That brings me to an explanation of how these books are structured. HealthScouter books include a number of what we call patient comments. These patient comments are summaries of what people have experienced. They're first hand accounts of what you may expect. These experiences effectively help you "catch up," and understand what outcomes are possible. They expose you to the treatments are available, and provide insight as to potential outcomes. They help you understand what other people are doing. So if you find yourself stuck feeling like you're receiving substandard medical care—or if you need a push to broach the subject, you can take this book to your provider and say, "Hey, I read here that another patient had this treatment—is that an option for me? If not, Why?" I believe that other peoples' experience is the most valuable way for you to formulate and build a list of good questions for your healthcare providers.

That notion is at the core of the HealthScouter philosophy.

So HealthScouter, by providing patient comments about a particular medical condition, will help expose you to what other people have experienced about a particular medical problem. If you know what other people have experienced, you can better understand what your options are. You'll be better informed and you'll have some questions to ask—it'll be like you've had access to dozens of other people who have gone through the same thing you're going through. And so armed, maybe you'll be able to move through your condition and get back on the road to health, and maybe you'll be able to do this with more grace than I have. And that is my sincere wish.

It's also my wish that perhaps when a doctor or nurse sees this little blue book, that they'll think twice about the care they're about to provide—knowing that the owner is a little bit better prepared, a little bit better armed—and yes, maybe even downright assertive.

I hope this book helps.

Yours truly,

Jim Stewart

San Diego, California

# HOW TO USE THIS BOOK

The purpose of HealthScouter is to help you understand your medical condition as quickly and easily as possible. We believe this can best be accomplished by reading about other people and their experiences negotiating their health and care. We try to leave out complicated medical jargon. And we've spent a considerable amount of time structuring this book so that it's easy to use. It's important to know that this is not the sort of book you read from beginning to end. Of course you may do so, but this book is more meaningful if you flip through quickly and scan for applicable material. Again, it's all about the patient commentary: The darkly shaded comments 🔳 indicate one patient initiating a new discussion, and the light or clear comments 🔲 are other comments associated with that same condition. So you should begin by looking for information from other patients who are experiencing the same aspect of the same medical condition that you studying. You can do this quickly by scanning through the book, focusing on the dark shaded comment boxes. By scanning the patient comments you'll find information about various aspects of a condition, all grouped together, in an easy-to-read format. In this way you can immediately begin reading about other

patients and their experiences with your particular
medical condition – and you can benefit immediately
from their experiences.

# INTRODUCTION TO MEDICAL CANNABIS

Medical cannabis (commonly referred to as "medical marijuana") refers to the use of the *Cannabis* plant as a physician-recommended drug or herbal therapy, as well as synthetic tetrahydrocannabinol (THC) and other cannabinoids. There are many studies regarding the use of cannabis in a medicinal context.[2][3] Use generally requires a prescription, and distribution is usually done within a framework defined by local laws. There are several methods for administration of dosage, including vaporizing or smoking dried buds, drinking or eating extracts, and taking synthetic THC pills.[4][5] The comparable efficacy of these methods was the subject of an investigative study by the National Institutes of Health.[3]

Medicinal use of cannabis is legal in a limited number of territories worldwide, including Canada, Austria, the Netherlands, Spain, Israel, Finland, and Portugal. In the United States, 13 states have recognized medical marijuana: Alaska, California, Colorado, Hawaii, Maine, Maryland, Michigan, Montana, Nevada, New Mexico, Oregon, Rhode Island, Vermont and Washington;[6][7] although California, Colorado, New Mexico and Rhode Island are currently the only states to utilize "dispensaries" to sell medical cannabis.

Seven U.S. states are currently considering medical marijuana bills in their legislatures: Illinois, Pennsylvania, Minnesota, New Hampshire, New Jersey, New York and North Carolina.[8] South Dakota also has several petitions in interest of medical marijuana legalization.[9]

Cannabis has a long history of medicinal use in many cultures. The U.S. federal government, as represented by the Department of Health and Human Services, holds a patent for medical marijuana.[10] Yet, medical cannabis remains a controversial issue worldwide. The Supreme Court ruled in 2005 that the Commerce Clause of the U.S. Constitution allowed the government to ban the use of cannabis, including medical use; the Food and Drug Administration states that "marijuana... has no currently accepted medical use in treatment in the United States".[11]

# PARTIAL LIST OF CLINICAL APPLICATIONS

Medical cannabis specialist Dr. Tod H. Mikuriya recorded over 250 indications for medical cannabis,[13] as classified by the International Statistical Classification of Diseases and Related Health Problems (ICD-9).[14]

In a 2002 review of medical literature, medical cannabis was shown to have established effects in the treatment of nausea, vomiting, premenstrual syndrome, unintentional weight loss, and lack of appetite. Other "relatively well-confirmed" effects were in the treatment of "spasticity, painful conditions, especially neurogenic pain, movement disorders, asthma, [and] Glaucoma".[15]

Preliminary findings indicate that cannabis-based drugs could prove useful in treating inflammatory bowel disease (consisting of Crohn's disease and ulcerative colitis),[16] migraines, fibromyalgia, and related conditions.[17]

Medical cannabis has also been found to relieve certain symptoms of multiple sclerosis[18] and spinal cord injuries[19][20][21][22] by exhibiting antispasmodic and muscle-relaxant properties as well as stimulating appetite. Clinical trials provide evidence that THC reduces motor and vocal tics of Tourette syndrome and related behavioral problems such as obsessive–compulsive disorders.[23][24]

Other studies have shown cannabis to be useful in treating alcoholism,[25] attention-deficit hyperactivity disorder(ADHD or AD/HD)[26][27] amyotrophic lateral sclerosis,[28][29][30] collagen-induced arthritis,[31] rheumatoid arthritis,[32] asthma,[33] atherosclerosis[34] autism,[35] bipolar disorder,[36][37][38] childhood mental disorders,[39] colorectal cancer,[40] depression,[41][42][43][44] diabetic retinopathy,[45][46][47] dystonia,[48][49] epilepsy,[50] digestive diseases,[51][52] gliomas,[53][54] hepatitis C,[55][56] Huntington's disease,[57] hypertension,[58][59] urinary incontinence,[60] leukemia,[61] skin tumors,[62][63] morning sickness,[64][65] methicillin-resistant *Staphylococcus aureus* (MRSA),[66][67][68] Parkinson's disease,[69] pruritus,[70][71] posttraumatic stress disorder (PTSD),[72][73][74] sickle-cell disease,[75] and sleep apnea.[76][77]

> *Some years ago I was diagnose with Paroxysmal hemicranias / ice pick headaches. I've found the worst of it is when I am doing strenuous exercise but get the outbreaks near 20 times a day now as it has been getting worst. The doctor has prescribed Topomax and indomethacin but we didn't have luck with Topomax and indomethacin made me vomit during exercise. At some point*

*I broke my hand playing soccer and they prescribed me Tramadol for that and that seemed to help the headaches somewhat. Now after taking this for more than a year I've found I need to take more and more of it for it to work and I have withdrawals when I don't take it and the headaches get worst.*

*I live in Michigan and they just passed the new law for medical marijuana use. I was curious if anyone was successful treating these headaches with marijuana, wondered if it'd work good enough to get me through my workout as I can't play soccer or workout anymore until I get something figured out.*

*Has anyone tried acupuncture or homeopathy for their gastroparesis? I went to an acupuncturist for 12 sessions, but it didn't seem to help. I can tell you what helps me though-- drinking wine. It eases any stomach pain I have, relaxes me, and increases my appetite. Again, I don't know if that's odd or not, but it works for me. I compare it to the husband of a friend of mine-- he has gastroparesis related to his diabetes and he has a prescription for medical marijuana which helps stimulate his appetite. I think of wine as stimulating mine. Then again, I've heard that alcohol actually SLOWS gastric emptying, so I don't know what to think.*

*I was looking into these clinical trials that you see for RSD and I'm seeing what anyone thinks about those if it's worth a risk. I have read that marijuana does help with RSD only problem is it's not medical use legal here in Illinois yet it's almost legal -- it passed the House vote.*

*I was diagnosed 15 years ago with Stage IV thyroid cancer, and given a 50% chance of surviving six months. Marijuana makes treatment and cancer more survivable. It has been shown to destroy many types of cancer cells. You will still have to have treatment, but it will be less horrible if you use marijuana.*

*Has anyone had success with treating bone cancer? I have stage IV breast cancer that metastasized to the bones- spine, hips, etc. I am on Taxol, Herceptin, and Zometa and want to learn more about hemp oil. I live in Colorado- so I can get a permit. But I don't know the first thing about getting started. Smoking it makes me ill. Will ingesting it help with my bones? I am willing to try but need some guidance.*

## Alzheimer's Disease

Research done by the Scripps Research Institute in California shows that the active ingredient in marijuana, THC, prevents the formation of deposits in the brain associated with Alzheimer's disease. THC was found to prevent an enzyme called acetylcholinesterase from accelerating the formation of "Alzheimer plaques" in the brain more effectively than commercially marketed drugs. THC is also more effective at blocking clumps of protein that can inhibit memory and cognition in Alzheimer's patients, as reported in Molecular Pharmaceutics.[78][79]

## Neuron Growth

A Canadian study shows marijuana promotes neuron growth. The Neuropsychiatry Research Unit at the University of Saskatchewan suggests the drug could have some benefits when administered regularly in a highly potent form. Whereas most "social drugs" such as alcohol, heroin, cocaine and nicotine suppress growth of new brain cells, the researchers found that cannabinoids promoted generation of new neurons in rats' hippocampi. The study held true for either plant-derived or synthetic versions of cannabinoids. The findings were published in the 2005 November issue of the Journal of Clinical Investigation.[80]

## Lung Cancer and COPD

THC has been found to reduce tumor growth in common lung cancer by 50 percent and to significantly reduce the ability of the cancer to spread, say researchers at Harvard University, who tested the chemical in both lab and mouse studies. The researchers suggest that THC might be used in a targeted fashion to treat lung cancer.[81]

In 2006, Donald Tashkin, M.D., of the University of California in Los Angeles, presented the results of his study, *Marijuana Use and Lung Cancer: Results of a Case-Control Study*. Tashkin found that smoking marijuana does not appear to increase the risk of lung cancer or head-and-neck malignancies, even among heavy users. The more tobacco a person smoked, the greater their risk of developing lung cancer and other cancers of the head and neck. But people who smoked more marijuana were not at increased risk compared with people who smoked less and people who didn't smoke at all.[82] Marijuana use was associated with cancer risk ratios below 1.0, indicating that a history of pot smoking had no effect on the risk for respiratory cancers. In contrast, tobacco smoking had a 21-fold risk for cancer. Tashkin concluded, "It's possible that tetrahydrocannabinol (THC) in marijuana smoke may encourage apoptosis, or programmed cell death, causing cells to die off before they have a chance to undergo malignant transformation".[83][84]

Similar findings were released in April 2009 by the Vancouver Burden of Obstructive Lung Disease Research Group. The study presents that smoking both tobacco and marijuana synergistically increased the risk of respiratory symptoms and COPD. Smoking only marijuana, however, was not associated with an increased risk of respiratory symptoms of COPD.[85][86] In a related commentary, Dr. Donald Tashkin writes that "we can be close to concluding that marijuana smoking by itself does not lead to COPD".[87]

*My mom's cancer has decided to grow again. She's suffering so much! The oncologist has referred her for radiation as she coughs constantly and has so much phlegm that she can't rest. She's also had these debilitating headaches... she's suffered from headaches for the last 15 or more years but they always stayed in the 3–5 pain level and now they're like a 10–12 so the doctor prescribed morphine and methadone. She thinks the cancer and headaches are related - I doubt it - she also said that mom had evidence of several small aneurisms but we've NEVER been told this before. She doesn't have the headaches as bad now but she's almost* incoherent. She doesn't want chemotherapy because she suffers bad side effects on everything they've tried and we're desperate to try and better her final days or months but now I don't know. Has anyone else heard or had experience with headaches associated with NSCLC? Does anyone have any ideas on what to do to help her? Does medical marijuana in the pill form help better? Would hospice be better for her now or would you think we should wait a little longer?

I am assuming that your mom has had a head CT and does not have brain medications? That could be causing headaches. My mom never complained about headaches during her battle with NSCLC.

From the experience we had with my mom I would say go ahead and get Hospice involved now as if they are anything like the hospice people we dealt with they are a blessing. They are very good at handling pain and making the person comfortable. Getting them does not mean the person is going to die today or the next or even the next month but rather that you are putting comfort and quality of life where it belongs, which in my book is #1. The hospice doctor assigned to my mom's case was a gem I only wish all doctors could be like him.

*If you have not read the book called Final Gifts by Maggie Callanan and Patricia Kelly I really recommend it for you and others in your family as it will help you deal with this part of the journey. They were hospice nurses and their book is great reading for anyone that has a loved one nearing the end of life for whatever reasons.*

## Breast Cancer

According to a 2007 study by scientists at the California Pacific Medical Center Research Institute, a compound found in cannabis may stop breast cancer from spreading throughout the body.[88][89] The scientists believe their discovery may provide a non-toxic alternative to chemotherapy while achieving the same results minus the painful and unpleasant side effects. The research team says that cannabidiol or CBD works by blocking the activity of a gene called Id-1, which is believed to be responsible for a process called metastasis, which is the aggressive spread of cancer cells away from the original tumor site.[90]

## HIV/AIDS

Investigators at Columbia University published clinical trial data in 2007 showing that HIV/AIDS patients who inhaled cannabis four times daily experienced substantial increases in food intake with little evidence of discomfort and no impairment of cognitive performance. They concluded that smoked marijuana has a clear medical benefit in HIV-positive patients.[91][92] In another study in 2008, researchers at the University of California, San Diego School of Medicine found that marijuana significantly reduces HIV-related neuropathic pain when added to a patient's already-prescribed pain management regimen and may be an "effective option for pain relief" in those whose pain is not controlled with current medications. Mood disturbance, physical disability, and quality of life all improved significantly during study treatment.[93][94] No serious adverse effects were reported, according to the study published by the American Academy of Neurology.[95]

## Brain Cancer

A study by Complutense University of Madrid found the active chemical in marijuana promotes the death of brain cancer cells by essentially helping them feed upon themselves in a process called autophagy. The research team discovered that cannabinoids such as THC had anticancer effects in mice with human brain cancer cells and in people with brain tumors. When mice with the human brain cancer cells received the THC, the tumor shrank. Using electron microscopes to analyze brain tissue taken both before and after a 26- to 30-day THC treatment regimen, the researchers found that THC eliminated cancer cells while leaving healthy cells intact.[96] The patients did not have any toxic effects from the treatment; previous studies of THC for the treatment of cancer have also found the therapy to be well tolerated. However, the mechanisms which promote THC's tumor cell–killing action are unknown.[97]

The researchers believe their findings may have therapeutic implications in the treatment of cancer, as detailed in their study, *Cannabinoid action induces autophagy-mediated cell death through stimulation of ER stress in human glioma cells,*[98] which appeared in the April 2009 issue of the Journal of Clinical Investigation.

## Head Injuries

Medical Marijuana (MMJ) has been shown to display neuroprotective properties with the 2-Arachidonoyl glycerol compound. This compound has been shown in lab experiments with mice to lower the amount of secondary damages from head injuries and speed up recovery time and effectiveness.[99]

## Opioid Dependence

Injections of THC eliminate dependence on opiates in stressed rats, according to a research team at the *Laboratory for Physiopathology of Diseases of the Central Nervous System (France) in the journal Neuropsychopharmacology.*[100] Deprived of their mothers at birth, rats become hypersensitive to the rewarding effect of morphine and heroin (substances belonging to the opiate family), and rapidly become dependent. When these rats were administered THC, they no longer developed typical morphine-dependent behavior. In the striatum, a region of the brain involved in drug dependence, the production of endogenous enkephalins was restored under THC, whereas it diminished in rats stressed from birth which had not received THC. The findings were released July 2009.[101] Researchers believe the findings could lead to therapeutic alternatives to existing substitution treatments.[102]

In humans, drug treatment subjects who use cannabis intermittently are found to be more likely to adhere to treatment for opioid dependence, according to clinical trial data published in the July/August 2009 issue of *American Journal on Addictions.*[103] Historically, similar findings were reported by Dr. Clendinning, who in 1843 utilized cannabis substitution for the treatment of alcoholism and opium addiction[104] and Dr. Birch, in 1889, who reported success in treating opiate and chloral addiction with cannabis.[105]

*Marijuana is definitely medicine!!! I wore Duragesic patches plus 180 a month 12.5 mg Hydrocodone (specially formulated). I am now down to 160 10 mg a month of Hydrocodone (40 a week). I still need the pain pills, but I am no longer the vegetable that I was turning into. I had a pain management doctor for a couple of years that just kept making the opiate narcotics stronger and stronger, yet if I were to have come up dirty for weed, he would have cut me off the narcotics. I don't know that my pain is bearable, but I do know that it will get nothing but worse. My back is never going to get better, only worse. I have just adjusted my life to fit around my disability. I stay laying down as much as possible, with my back leaning at an angle into a bunch of pillows. I also have a magnificent, miracle service dog named Mogi.*

*My regular doctor has now started prescribing for me and he too is amazed that I have cut down on the narcotics. My doctor now, not only prescribes my Marinol, but also my marijuana. Unfortunately, in the state of Alaska, I have no*

*access to weed except to buy it or to grow it.
Living on SSI, buying is a little out of the question.
I am only allowed six plants at a time, with only
three in bud... Not nearly enough. I live in the
Mat-Su Valley, home of Matanuska Thunderfuck.
We have the longest growing season for outdoors
of anyplace in the USA. I grow inside, though,
because there are just too many variables to
have my plants outside. This summer, I tried
having plants outside when my daylight was 24
hours, but I am worried that I left them out too
long and very worried about fungus gnats, etc. I
didn't bring them in until the daylight was down
to about 15 hours, then I had to bug bomb the
shit out of them, then I had to shape them after
letting them go all summer outside. I don't think I
will do this again. I like to have more control over
my plants, especially since I am only allowed to
have so few. It is absolutely not worth getting in
trouble for, that's for sure. I am at home all the
time and live out in the woods.*

| Indication | Benefit |
|---|---|
| Alzheimer's | Prevents formation of "Alzheimer plaques" |
| Arthritis | Analgesic, anti-inflammatory |
| Asthma | Opens up airways in lungs |

| Brain Cancer | Reduces tumors, kills cancer cells |
|---|---|
| Breast Cancer | Stops cancer from spreading |
| Depression | Brightens mood |
| Glaucoma | Reduces eye pressure |
| Head Injuries | Neuroprotective properties, speeds recovery time |
| HIV | Reduces neuropathic pain, improves appetite and sleep |
| Hypertension | Lowers blood pressure |
| Lung Cancer | Reduces tumors, slows cancer growth |
| Pain | Non-opiate, non-addictive pain killer |
| A.D.D. | Regulates the effects of A.D.D. |

## Chronic Pain

*I wake up EVERY night because of back and neck pain. I take a pain pill and try to get back to sleep. I can almost never get back to sleep. The exception is the Cannabis edible. I make them very strong so one cookie will work better than ANY sleeping pill. I say this with absolute confidence. Yes I know people that tell me I should be "wasted" taking that much pain medicine. I don't get any thrill from pills. I barely feel any reduction in pain as it is.*

*Anyone who knows me knows I hate taking pills. I also know that if one pill doesn't work then 4–5 won't do it either. I go the other way with my pain pills. When I am fortunate enough to have a harvest I make edibles. They help me like nothing else can. When I do have these I am able to REDUCE the Oxycontin. I usually take half pills when I am eating edibles. Then when I am out of edibles I can take my regular dose of pain pills and they work a little bit better because I have been taking less for a certain time.*

*I have had antidepressants pushed on me every time I go to my appointments. I have tried them in the past but they do nothing for me. Cannabis is my antidepressant. I think doctors push way too many drugs on people period.*

*I'm suffering from terrific pain in my muscles and bones from the disease LUPUS. I am finding great relief from cannabis, especially from muscle spasms. Pain can leave a person feeling very depressed and cannabis helps that too.*

*Until you are deep into it, you just don't realize how constant chronic pain can affect your life. I am a middle aged man with a wife and kids. I was the sole provider for our family before an*

*accident left me with a titanium plate in my neck, partial paralysis, mobility issues, and CONSTANT PAIN. Over the years I have tried different pain medications and am currently taking Oxycontin @ 160 mg a day, valium, and Trazadone. The side effects from these drugs are the pits. They really mess up your body and you become physically addicted to them.*

*Cannabis has really saved my life. One of the other problems I have is terrible insomnia because of the pain. The ONLY way I am able to get a solid night's sleep is with the aid of a cannabis edible. I have tried smoking it and it works to a certain degree, but edibles work best for me. One cannabis cookie can take the place of an 80 mg Oxycontin pill. About a year ago when I wanted to stop the pain medications I was able to stop completely for one week with the aid of cannabis edibles.*

*Cannabis also helps me with depression. Being disabled and not being able to work or provide for my family has left me with lots of different emotions that I really don't care to have. I feel like a loser for not being able to work, and now my wife has to take care of our family. I feel like a loser when I can't do the things other fathers can do with their kids. I feel like I have let my family down when bills keep adding up. I feel like it's just not fair the hand I was dealt. I worked like a dog for over 25 years only to be brought to my knees. I feel like a loser... but cannabis puts it into perspective for me. I will do the best I can and I do have the love and support of my family.*

*I live in California and have had a prescription for six years. My mother who is 65 and was always against any kind of marijuana is now a cannabis user. Suffering with bi-polar depression for 40+ years, used every med available, electro-shock treatments... she now has found relief with cannabis.*

## Stress and Mental Health

*I have a close friend who suffers from PTSD and he reports major benefits using cannabis over pharmaceuticals (indica strains in particular - think it may have something to do with the CBD levels). His father passed away in front of him and he attempted to save his life. He was only a senior in high school (all he had to his name was a car that wasn't paid for yet), his mother left and didn't want much to do with him, so*

*he had a lot of responsibilities thrown on his shoulders all at once, on top of losing his father. He had been unsuccessfully treated with several prescription drugs since he was in high school all the way up until two years after he graduated high school and stumbled upon cannabis. Now he's in his mid 30's now on no pharmaceutical drugs doing just fine.*

*What I like about MMJ is that it doesn't make me forget my trauma like it never happened at all. It just makes it so I can remember my traumatic events when I choose to remember them and deal with them on my own terms like I would deal with any normal event.*

*It would be bad just to forget trauma completely, because then how could people prevent future traumas?*

*I think there's a misunderstanding about pot where people think it makes you too numb to feel or too confused to remember and that's how it "helps."*

*But it's the PTSD that causes the numbness and confusion. Medical marijuana cures the numbness and confusion and opens the window of feeling* and clarity through which one can heal and grow.

I hope enlightenment on this subject can spread more rapidly. I feel anxious for all those soldiers trying to defend their lives and their sanity from intrusive memories that are overpowering them and keeping them from living as whole people.

And what about law enforcement? It's tragic that the police are so determined to bully the potheads, when law enforcement officers suffer terrible PTSD from the awful things they have to witness on the job.

That's the real tragic irony here. They do suffer a lot. Yet they're fighting so hard against the medicine they need the most.

Look at the DEA. They're obsessed with their traumatic memories. A lot of agents get tortured and killed in the process of their work. The DEA is filled with PTSD.

Yet here they are, fighting angrily, with rage, against a natural anti-traumatic.

Maybe they're caught in the awful corner where they think relinquishing their PTSD would be *disloyal to the victims? They turn their trauma into a shrine to the victims of the war they support themselves by fighting.*

*It's sad.*

*I'm grateful I've been able to heal my own trauma with medical marijuana.*

*I wish the DEA could understand the vicious circle they've caught themselves in -- getting PTSD while making a living fighting a war over an herb that cures PTSD.*

*Although I also have chronic pain from interstitial cystitis and fibromyalgia, technically my medical marijuana recommendation is for DID, which is like an extreme version of PTSD. It's like PTSD so bad that you forget who you are even.*

*I would say based on my one person clinical trial, medical marijuana works pretty well. I haven't woken up with a horrible nightmare about being abused since I started using medical marijuana. I don't hold my keys in my hand ready to lash out at an attacker in the mall any more. And I don't organize all my thoughts about life around my past trauma any more.*

My doctor considers this experiment in using pot to heal a trauma victim a huge success.

There is much scientific evidence accruing in animal studies that PTSD is actually CAUSED by damage to the CB1 receptor -- by genetic means and/or exposure to real life trauma that causes stress chemicals called glutamates to singe the hippocampus.

Part of PTSD is the inability to screen your memories. You can't keep the past in the past. The past keeps taking over your present against your will.

The CB1 receptor plays a crucial role in the ability to keep the past in the past. That's the short term memory thing. Forgetting is an important part of living. That's why we make a drug in our own minds that aids forgetting.

PTSD is a disorder of forgetting. You can't forget what you need to forget in order to live in the NOW. That means the part of the brain that helps you forget has been harmed. That natural forgetting drug in your brain isn't doing its job.

That's what they're finding in animal research on PTSD. The scientists block the CB1 receptor and *the mice can't forget even the most minor slightly painful stimuli that doesn't bother the mice whose CB1 receptors were not blocked.*

*If you want to keep up with the latest research, try Googling "PTSD cannabinoids" or "PTSD CB1" -- stuff like that.*

*This is the area where medical marijuana becomes the most politically threatening to the mainstream. Trauma is often politically induced. The people on the bottom get the most trauma.*

*I think this is true root of the evil tree of marijuana prohibition. During the 1920s, people expected blacks to act like PTSD victims and shrink from eye contact with white people out of fear.*

*The famous racist quote from the Hearst paper -- "Reefer makes a darkie look a white man in the eye" -- could be seen as an early testament to both the power of medical marijuana to treat PTSD, and the power of the white middle class mainstream to ban medical marijuana for that reason.*

*Imagine how threatened and outraged and fearful a white racist in 1920 would feel around black people who had forgotten their fear of the Master.*

*A healed trauma victim is politically more effective -- and hence more dangerous to the perpetrator of the trauma -- than a trauma victim still being controlled by fear from the past.*

*Medical marijuana helps me live a normal life. I haven't had a heart palpitation in a long time. It helps me calm down so I don't go into anxiety overdrive and worry myself to depression. I can't say enough how much it has helped me. I've held a job recently much longer than I've been able to in a long time thanks for medicating. I don't take any synthetic medication- just medical marijuana. And I don't need anything else. It even relieves my horrible monthly girl cramps.*

*I have suffered from anxiety and depression for years and have been hospitalized as being suicidal four times in the last five years. My hospital stays have lasted between 3–13 days each. I have taken every anti-anxiety and depression medicine imaginable, including Saroquil, Lithium, Cymbalta, Celexa, Clonozapan, MAOI's, etc. As I am currently on disability for my condition, a good portion of my medications have been paid for through my Medicaid prescription plan, but you can bet that tens of thousands of dollars have been spent to keep me "stable" in the last five years.*

*Side effects I have experienced with prescribed medications, included (depending on the drug); being and a continuous "dazed" state of mind, nightmares (waking up actually hitting my wife or the wall with my hands), heartburn, increased appetite, decreased appetite, sleepiness and confusion, not to mention the wear and tear on my liver, pancreas and kidneys from assorted drugs.*

*A few months ago, I decided that I was fed up with the side effects of my most recent medications and chose to wean myself off of them. As I was still struggling with the anxiety after I got of the medications, I had a friend suggest that I use medical marijuana in a strictly medical capacity. I tried it and the results were amazing! I have been much calmer, able to focus and I do not "obsess" over things like I did before.*

*I went to my family doctor (whom I have seen for 20 years) and told him of my experience, in* response, he told me that he had been concerned about the effects of the drugs I had been taking and enthusiastically encouraged me to continue to use medical marijuana. As I am in a state that does not have a "legalized" program, he gave me some good advice:

1. Don't tell anybody I am using.

2. Be careful where I get it.

3. Don't drive while using (just like many of my other prescribed medications)

4. Don't carry it with me.

5. Only use it when I feel I really need it.

6. Only use small quantities, as larger quantities are counterproductive to the desired effect.

I have been using the medical marijuana, as prescribed and my anxiety is now under control. As my major depressive episodes were triggered by extreme anxiety, my depression is currently in remission.

However, my wife has a big problem with me using medical marijuana simply because it is not legal. The funny thing is that over the years *she has practically crammed the medications--that turned me into a zombie and had bad side effects--down my throat, but now that I found something that REALLY works, she is not supportive due to the legal aspects of this issue.*

*Also, I have taken medical costs from close to $2,000 a month, down to less than $100, saving Medicaid (and thus the American Tax Payer), significant amounts of money.*

*I am currently using medical marijuana and strictly following my doctor's guidelines. I would advise anybody who suffers from severe anxiety to try medical marijuana, keeping in mind that small doses work wonders and large doses are counterproductive and can create problems. Also, when you get a new bag, start with VERY SMALL doses, until you are familiar with the potency.*

*I hope this information about my experiences will help others who have lived with anxiety-caused depression, just be careful. Be smart. Be responsible. Use it as a medicine and not as an "escape" and continue with therapy.*

*I've had severe anxiety and depression my whole life. I used alcohol to get through college* and most of my 20s. I was taught and believed all the lies about MJ. I finally sought help and was put on a series of anti-depressants that did nothing for me, except Luvox made me twitch uncontrollably. The Ativan helped a lot, especially to sleep, but it's hard to get Doctors to prescribe it because it's "addictive". When I moved to CA, I learned about medical marijuana and finally decided to try it. I had tried marijuana before but it just made me more anxious. Once I realized that it wasn't evil and I actually had a prescription for it that made it as legal as all those anti-depressants I was on, I could smoke and it really helped. My problem right now, and what I'm asking advice for, is that I was then diagnosed as Bipolar and have been on a string of Bipolar medications, all that have caused worse symptoms like gaining 40lbs overnight even though I ate a good diet and exercised. Then on another one I lost all the weight but I was so tired I couldn't make it out of bed except to lay on the couch. I've just weaned myself off of it and I know my Psychiatrist is going to be mad but it takes forever just to get in to see him and if you need to get off a med you are SOL. I don't know whether to let him put me on another one when I see him again. I'd really like to only use medical marijuana and Ativan. I'm worried though that what they call my manic episodes will return and I don't want that. I've read that MMJ does help bipolar but the last doctor who gave me my renewed prescription wouldn't give it to me for bipolar, anxiety, or depression. She wrote it for pain, which is true, I hurt my back really bad and it's always been painful, but the other anxiety, etc. is what has always held me back and what I really need it for. She said there was no medical evidence and she could not and would not prescribe it to me for that. The only reason I did get it renewed (I had moved to northern California and had to find a new doctor that prescribed MMJ) was because on the background info it asked if I had ever been in any accidents and I had which resulted in the pain. Does anyone know of or have any experiences that can help me with this decision? I need all the help I can get because I've decided not to take medications before and the psychiatrist easily talked me into trying a new drug.

# MEDICINAL COMPOUNDS

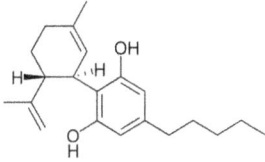

Cannabidiol has many positive effects.

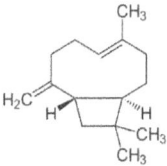

β-Caryophyllene has important anti-inflammatory properties.

## Cannabidiol

Cannabidiol, also known as "CBD", is a major constituent of medical cannabis. CBD represents up to 40% of extracts of the medical cannabis plant.[106] Cannabidiol relieves convulsion, inflammation, anxiety, nausea, and inhibits cancer cell growth.[107] Recent studies have shown cannabidiol to be as effective as atypical antipsychotics in treating schizophrenia.[108] In November 2007 it was reported that CBD reduces growth of aggressive human breast cancer cells *in vitro* and reduces their invasiveness. It thus represents the first non-toxic exogenous agent that can lead to down-regulation of tumor aggressiveness.[109][110] It is also a neuroprotective antioxidant.[111]

## β-Caryophyllene

Part of the mechanism by which medical cannabis has been shown to reduce tissue inflammation is via a compound called β-caryophyllene.[112] A cannabinoid receptor called CB2 plays a vital part in reducing inflammation in humans and other animals.[112] β-Caryophyllene has been shown to be a selective activator of the CB2 receptor.[112] β-Caryophyllene is especially concentrated in cannabis essential oil, which contains about 12–35% β-caryophyllene.[112]

# PHARMACOLOGIC THC AND THC DERIVATIVES

In the USA, the FDA has approved two cannabinoids for use as medical therapies: dronabinol (Marinol) and nabilone. It is important to note that these medicines are not smoked. Dronabinol is a synthetic THC medication,[113] while nabilone is a synthetic cannabinoid marketed under the brand name Cesamet.

These medications are usually used when first line treatments for nausea fail to work. In extremely high doses and in rare cases there is a possibility of "psychotomimetic" side effects. The other commonly-used antiemetic drugs are not associated with these side effects.

The prescription drug Sativex, an extract of cannabis administered as a sublingual spray, has been approved in Canada for the adjunctive treatment (use alongside other medicines) of both multiple sclerosis[114] and cancer related pain.[115] This medication may now be legally imported into the United Kingdom and Spain on prescription.[116] Dr. William Notcutt is one of the chief researchers that has developed Sativex, and he has been working with GW and founder Geoffrey Guy since the company's inception in 1998. Notcutt states that the use of MS as the disease to study "had everything to do with politics."[117]

Scientists are also working on drugs that prevent naturally occurring enzymes from blocking pain-relieving cannabinoid receptors such as 2-arachidonoylgylcerol (2-AG).[118]

| Medication | Year approved | Licensed indications | Cost |
|---|---|---|---|
| Nabilone | 1985 | Nausea of cancer chemotherapy that has failed to respond adequately to other antiemetics | $4000.00 U.S. for a year's supply (in Canada)[119] |
| Marinol | 1992 | Nausea of cancer chemotherapy that has failed to respond adequately to other antiemetics, AIDS wasting | $723.16 U.S. for 30 doses @ 10 mg online[120] |
| Sativex | 1995, 1997 | The product is approved in Canada as adjunctive treatment for the symptomatic relief of neuropathic pain in multiple sclerosis, and more recently for pain due to cancer. Extracted from cannabis plants. | $9,351 Canadian per year[121] |

*I have been with cannabis since 2000. I have suffered from many ailments before being told that I had MS. For eight years I had been drug dependent and homebound due to my agoraphobia. When I found out that I had MS, my husband and caregiver had worked with many doctors with this ailment, and then found a doctor that recommended cannabis. Once I started using cannabis, I was able to release most of the pharmaceutical drugs that I depended upon step-by-step, year by year, and soon I was able to let go the use of my wheelchair on short distances. Now I am able to walk using a walker on certain days, and my cane on others. I know that cannabis has worked for me and I am grateful to being part of society again even with my challenges that I face due to my illness. I am really glad that this was available to me, and it has changed my life. I am still unable to work, but now I am able to do things I could not do before. That is living life.*

MEDICAL CANNABIS

# HISTORY OF CANNABIS

The use of cannabis, at least as fiber, has been shown to go back at least 10,000 years in Taiwan. "Dà má" (Pinyin pronunciation) is the Chinese expression for cannabis, the first character meaning "big" and the second character meaning "hemp."

Cannabis, called dà má (大麻) in Chinese, is known to have been used in Taiwan for fiber starting about 10,000 years ago.[122] Cannabis has been used for medicinal purposes for approximately 4,000 years.[123] In the early 3rd century AD, Hua Tuo was the first known person in China to use cannabis as an anesthetic. He reduced the plant to powder and mixed it with wine for administration.[124] Cannabis was prescribed to treat vomiting, plus infectious and parasitic hemorrhaging. Cannabis is one of the 50 "fundamental" herbs in traditional Chinese medicine.[125]

## Ancient Egypt

The Ebers Papyrus (ca. 1,550 B.C.) from Ancient Egypt describes medical marijuana.[126] Other ancient Egyptian papyri that mention medical marijuana are the Ramesseum III Papyrus (1700 BC), the Berlin Papyrus (1300 BC) and the Chester Beatty Medical

Papyrus VI (1300 BC).[127] The ancient Egyptians even used hemp (cannabis) in suppositories for relieving the pain of hemorrhoids.[128] The Egyptologist Lise Manniche notes the reference to "plant medical marijuana" in several Egyptian texts, one of which dates back to the eighteenth century B.C.[129]

## Ancient India

Surviving texts from ancient India confirm that cannabis' psychoactive properties were recognized, and doctors used it for a variety of illnesses and ailments. These included insomnia, headaches, a whole host of gastrointestinal disorders, and pain: cannabis was frequently used to relieve the pain of childbirth.[130]

## Ancient Greece

The Ancient Greeks used cannabis not only for human medicine, but also for veterinary medicine.[131] The Greeks used cannabis to dress wounds and sores on their horses.[131]

In humans, dried leaves of cannabis were used to treat nose bleeds, and cannabis seeds were used to expel tapeworms.[131] The most frequently described use of cannabis in humans was to steep green seeds of cannabis in either water or wine, later taking the seeds out and using the warm extract to treat inflammation and pain resulting from obstruction of the ear.[131]

In the 5th century BCE Herodotus, a Greek historian, described how the Scythians of the Middle East used cannabis in steam baths.[131]

## Medieval Islamic World

In the medieval Islamic world, Arabic physicians made use of the diuretic, antiemetic, antiepileptic, anti-inflammatory, pain killing and antipyretic properties of *Cannabis sativa,* and used it extensively as medication from the 8th to 18th centuries.[132]

## Modern Science

An Irish doctor, William Brooke O'Shaughnessy, was held mainly responsible for showing his Western colleagues about the healing properties of cannabis. He was an herb professor at the Medical College of Calcutta, and conducted a cannabis experiment in the 1830s. O'Shaughnessy created preparations and tested animal effects. He continued on to administer it to patients in order to help treat muscle spasms/ stomach cramps or general pain.[133]

An advertisement for cannabis Americana distributed by a pharmacist in New York in 1917.

Cannabis as a medicine became common throughout much of the world by the 19th century. It was used as the primary pain reliever until the invention of aspirin.[123] Modern medical and scientific inquiry began with doctors like O'Shaughnessy and Moreau de Tours, who used it to treat melancholia and migraines, and as a sleeping aid, analgesic and anticonvulsant.

By the time the United States banned cannabis in a federal law, the 1937 Marijuana Tax Act, the plant was no longer extremely popular.[134] Skepticism about cannabis arose in response to the bill. The situation was exacerbated by the stereotypes promoted by the media, that the drug was used primarily by Mexican and African immigrants.[134]

Later in the century, researchers investigating methods of detecting cannabis intoxication discovered that smoking the drug reduced intraocular pressure.[135]

In 1972 Tod H. Mikuriya, M.D. reignited the debate concerning cannabis as medicine when he published "Marijuana Medical Papers." High intraocular pressure causes blindness in glaucoma patients, so many believed that using the drug could prevent blindness in patients. Many Vietnam War veterans also believed that the drug prevented muscle spasms caused by battle-induced spinal injuries.[136] Later medical use has focused primarily on its role in preventing the wasting syndromes and chronic loss of appetite associated with chemotherapy and AIDS, along with a variety of rare muscular and skeletal disorders. Less commonly, cannabis has been used in the treatment of alcoholism and addiction to other drugs such as heroin and the prevention of migraines. In recent years, studies have shown or researchers have speculated that the main chemical in the drug, THC, might help prevent atherosclerosis.

Later, in the 1970s, a synthetic version of THC, the primary active ingredient in cannabis, was synthesized to make the drug Marinol. Users reported several problems with Marinol, however, that led many to abandon the pill and resume smoking the plant. Patients complained that the violent nausea associated with chemotherapy made swallowing pills difficult. The effects of smoked cannabis are felt almost immediately, and is therefore easily dosed.[137] Marinol (Jojel), like ingested cannabis, is very psychoactive, and is harder to titrate than smoked cannabis.[138] Marinol has also consistently been more expensive than herbal cannabis.[139] Some studies have indicated that other chemicals in the plant may have a synergistic effect with THC.[140]

In addition, during the 1970s and 1980s, six U.S. states' health departments performed studies on the use of medical cannabis. These are widely considered some of the most useful and pioneering studies on the subject. Voters in eight states showed their support for cannabis prescriptions or recommendations given by physicians between 1996 and 1999, including Alaska, Arizona, California, Colorado, Maine, Michigan, Nevada, Oregon, and Washington, going against policies of the federal government.[141]

In May 2001, "The Chronic Cannabis Use in the Compassionate Investigational New Drug Program: An Examination of Benefits and Adverse Effects of Legal Clinical Cannabis" (Russo, Mathre, Byrne et al.) was completed. This three-day examination of major body functions of four of the five living US federal cannabis patients found "mild pulmonary changes" in two patients.[142]

On October 7, 2003 a patent entitled "Cannabinoids as Antioxidants and Neuroprotectants" (#6,630,507) was awarded to the United States Department of Health and Human Services, based on research done at the National Institute of Mental Health (NIMH), and the National Institute of Neurological Disorders and Stroke (NINDS). This patent claims that cannabinoids are "useful in the treatment and prophylaxis of wide variety of oxidation associated diseases, such as ischemic, age-related, inflammatory and autoimmune diseases. The cannabinoids are found to have particular application as neuroprotectants, for example in limiting neurological damage following ischemic insults, such as stroke and trauma, or in the treatment of neurodegenerative diseases, such as Alzheimer's disease, Parkinson's disease and HIV dementia."[143]

Historian Jacob Appel has argued that the medicinal cannabis movement bears striking similarities to the medicinal beer movement of the 1920s.[144] Both efforts attempted to muster medical expertise in the face of a national prohibition and both pitted the rights of physicians against the authority of the federal government.

*My husband was diagnosed with Parkinson's at the age of 75 and from his doctor friend whom*

*he was playing golf with. We lived in a Country Club and his friend notices that Howard was trembling and unable to swing his club as he had in the past. My husband played golf all around the world for his job as part of his job.*

*We began the long journey to the many doctors and clinics in Las Vegas and after selling our homes, we continued our "search for a cure" in Palm Springs. It was in Palm Springs that we found the "peace" my husband was seeking... He just wanted to stop the shaking! The medication my husband was given did absolutely nothing but make him drool at the dinner table and fall asleep in the oddest places. Nothing stopped the shaking; he was miserable and became very depressed.*

*It was mentioned by a friend to have him smoke a joint to see if that helped. Because my husband was brought up in the generation of scare tactics by the government through films like "Refer Madness", he would never even consider trying it, plus, he did not smoke. With that said, I took the liberty, as his wife and caregiver, to give him some without telling him. I watched him very closely as I had no idea how he would be affected and after 45 minutes he stopped shaking!! I walked over to his easy chair where he was watching GMA and I sat on the ottoman in front of him... I leaned into him and said, "Hey, how do you feel?" He looked at me with a happiness on his face that we had not seen for many months and put his two hands out in front of himself and said "Look! I'm not shaking!"... and he stopped shaking for six hours! He didn't want to move from his chair in fear this euphoria would end.*

*It was a moment I will never forget.*

*We then found a doctor who gave us a prescription and off we went to the dispensary in Palm Desert where we met with very knowledgeable young people who were thrilled to have my husband as a new patient. We had no idea of the fabulous eatables available for him such as peanut butter, cooking oil, candy, breads, chocolate and ice cream. We spent some $400 and became customers for the next two years of my husband's life.*

*Now I am not saying we found the cure for Parkinson's... however, we found relief from shaking, and as I have learned since my husband's death, at the age of 80 and in 2007,* the medical marijuana gave him a new lease on his quality of life. He was happy because he was not shaking!!

The new face of marijuana users are older American's seeking better options to the awful side effects of some of the pharmaceutical drugs that ruin your organs and for my husband's Parkinson's... none ever stopped the darn shaking!!

I have a lot to say about the health benefits of medical marijuana.

First I am a 46 year old mother of two. In 2006, I had suffered four strokes, all apparently related to Premarin, a hormone replacement therapy I had been prescribed after a hysterectomy in 2002.

At first, doctors explained that I would more than likely not stand for approximately six months. This was devastating news since my children relied on me for everything. I wasn't able to work, and an injury to my brain that not only left me immobile, it left me with huge emotional issues and depression. Any and all activity around me often left me over stimulated *and overwhelmed and unable to function. My thoughts were often random and completely unfocused. I spent 1.5 months in a rehabilitation hospital. Everything was controlled with medications that often left me more groggy and incoherent than I was already.*

*Spasticity was my greatest hurdle, when I walked I felt like the Tin Man needing some oil. A friend suggested I try medical marijuana for depression and spasms. What a big difference. My normal patterns of obsessing about my abilities were soon calm focused thoughts. Spasms were more tolerable and my movement became more fluid. No more tripping and falling, either. Endless nights of no sleep soon became quiet rest. I know that we struggle with the thought of allowing access of medical marijuana for those in need, but truly my life would not be as good as it is now nor would my children have a mother to care for them as they need.*

*I was up walking within four months, and I was driving a full size truck with manual transmission (five speed) within five months.*

*Although I have no use of my left arm/hand I still am able now to full dress and care for myself.*

*Medical marijuana has given me the quality I deserve.*

## Organizational Support

An increasing number of medical organizations have endorsed allowing patient's access to medical marijuana with their physicians' approval. These include, but are not limited to, the following:

• The American College of Physicians - America's second largest physicians group[145]

• Leukemia & Lymphoma Society - America's second largest cancer charity.[145]

• American Academy of Family Physicians[145]

• American Public Health Association[145]

• American Psychiatric Association[145]

• American Nurses Association[145]

• British Medical Association[145]

• AIDS Action[145]

• American Academy of HIV Medicine[145]

• Lymphoma Foundation of America[145]

• Health Canada[145]

- NORML[145]

- SSDP[145]

# CRITICISM

A major criticism of cannabis as medicine is opposition to smoking as a method of consumption.

On 20 April 2006, the United States Food and Drug Administration (FDA) issued an advisory against *smoked* medical marijuana stating that, "marijuana has a high potential for abuse, has no currently accepted medical use in treatment in the United States, and has a lack of accepted safety for use under medical supervision. Furthermore, there is currently sound evidence that smoked marijuana is harmful."[146] Some prominent American societies have been reluctant to endorse medicinal cannabis. For example:,[147] the National Multiple Sclerosis Society,[148] the American Academy of Ophthalmology[149] and the American Cancer Society.[150] (Federal Register, 1992).

The Institute of Medicine, run by the United States National Academy of Sciences, conducted a comprehensive study in 1999 to assess the potential health benefits of cannabis and its constituent cannabinoids. The study concluded that smoking cannabis is not recommended for the treatment of any disease condition, but did conclude that nausea, appetite loss, pain and anxiety can all be mitigated by marijuana. While the study expressed reservations about smoked marijuana due to the health risks associated with smoking, the study team concluded that until another mode of ingestion was perfected that could provide the same relief as smoked marijuana, there was no alternative. Modern vaporizers and the ingestion of cannabis in a decarboxylated state have laid most of these concerns to rest, however. In addition, the study pointed out the inherent difficulty in marketing a non patentable herb. Pharmaceutical companies will not substantially profit unless there is a patent. For those reasons, the Institute of Medicine concluded that there is little future in smoked cannabis as a medically approved medication. The report also concluded for certain patients, such as the terminally ill or those with debilitating symptoms, the long-term risks are not of great concern. Medical Marijuana Passes House Civil Justice Committee Without Dissent by David Guard (MARCH 11, 2009).[151]

In an unpublished 2001 study by the Mayo Clinic, Marinol was shown to be less effective than the steroid megestrol acetate in helping cancer patients regain lost appetites.[152] The mechanism by which megestrol acetate works is unknown and the compound can cause "impotence, gas, rash, high blood pressure, fever, decreased libido, insomnia, upset stomach, and high blood sugar...," as well as "breakthrough bleeding" in women.

## Harm Reduction

Many medical cannabis opponents note that smoking cannabis is harmful to the respiratory system. However, this harm can be minimized or eliminated by the use of a vaporizer or ingesting the drug in an edible form or other non-smoking modes of delivery like tinctures. Vaporizers are devices that vaporize the active constituents (cannabinoids) and the fragrant aromatic substances in the preparation without combusting the plant material and thus preventing the formation of toxic substances. Studies have shown that vaporizers can dramatically reduce[153] or even eliminate[154] the release of irritants and toxic compounds.

In order to kill microorganisms, especially mold, the scientists "Levitz and Diamond (1991) suggested baking marijuana in home ovens at 150°C [302°F], for five minutes before smoking. Oven treatment killed conidia of A. *fumigatus, A. flavus* and A. *niger,* and did not degrade the active component of marijuana, tetrahydrocannabinol (THC)".[155]

## Availability in Austria

On July 9, 2008 the Austrian Parliament approved cannabis cultivation for scientific and medical uses.[156]

## Availability in Canada

In Canada, the regulation on access to marijuana for medical purposes, established by Health Canada in July 2001, defines two categories of patients eligible for access to medical cannabis. The category 1 list individuals suffering from "acute pain", "violent nausea and/or other serious symptoms caused by the following conditions: multiple sclerosis, spinal cord injury, disease of the spinal cord, cancer, AIDS/HIV infection, severe forms of arthritis and/or epilepsy. The category 2 "key applicants who have serious pathological symptoms other than those described in category 1."[157] The application of eligible patients must be supported by a doctor.

The cannabis distributed by Health Canada is provided under the brand CannaMed by the company Prairie Plant Systems Inc. In 2006, 420 kg of CannaMed cannabis was sold, representing an increase of 80% over the previous year.[158] However, patients complain of the single strain selection as well as low potency, providing a pre-ground product put through a wood chipper (which deteriorates rapidly) as well as gamma irradiation and foul taste and smell. [159] It is also legal for patients approved by Health Canada to grow their own cannabis for personal consumption, and it is possible to obtain a production license as a person designated by a patient. This has been expanded by recent court rulings, and it is said[by whom?] that Health Canada's claim that "no notice of compliance has been issued for marijuana for medical purposes" is violating the human rights of medical marijuana patients. Advocates for marijuana use have stated that they will be launching a court case that would legalize marijuana use for both medicinal and recreational use.[160]

## Availability in Spain

In Spain, since the late 1990s and early 2000s, medical cannabis underwent a process of progressive decriminalization and legalization. The parliament of the region of Catalonia is the first in Spain have voted unanimously in 2001 legalizing medical marijuana, it is quickly followed by parliaments of Aragon and the Balearic Islands. The Spanish Penal Code prohibits the sale of cannabis but it does not prohibit consumption. Until early 2000, the Penal Code did not distinguish between therapeutic use of cannabis and recreational use, however, several court decisions show that this distinction is increasingly taken into account by the judges. From 2006, the sale of seed is legalized, possession or consumption is still forbidden in public places but permitted in private premises. Moreover, the cultivation of cannabis plants is now authorized in a private place.

Several studies have been conducted to study the effects of cannabis on patients suffering from diseases like cancer, AIDS, multiple sclerosis, seizures or asthma. This research was conducted by various Spanish agencies at the Universidad Complutense de Madrid headed by Dr. Manuel Guzman, the hospital of La Laguna in Tenerife led neurosurgeon Luis González Feria or the University of Barcelona.

After legislation, several cannabis clubs have been established including the Basque Country and Catalonia. These clubs, the first of its kind in Europe, are non-profit associations who grow cannabis and sell it at cost to its members. In 2006, members of these clubs were acquitted in trial for possession and sale of cannabis.

## Availability in United States

The use, sale and possession of cannabis (marijuana) in the United States are illegal under federal law.

However, some states have created exemptions for medical marijuana use. In July 2009, President Barack Obama's drug czar Gil Kerlikowske clarified the federal government's position when he stated that "marijuana is dangerous and has no medicinal benefit" and that "legalization is not in the president's vocabulary, and it's not in mine."[1]

# LEGAL HISTORY

Under federal law, it is illegal to possess, use, buy, sell, or cultivate marijuana, since the Controlled Substances Act of 1970 classifies marijuana as a Schedule I drug, claiming it has a high potential for abuse and has no acceptable medical use.

Some states and local governments have established laws attempting to decriminalize cannabis, which has reduced the number of "simple possession" offenders sent to jail, since federal enforcement agents rarely target individuals directly for such relatively minor offenses. Other state and local governments ask law enforcement agencies to limit enforcement of drug laws with respect to cannabis, however under the Supremacy Clause of the United States Constitution, federal law preempts conflicting state and local laws. In most cases, the absence of a state law does not present a preemption conflict with a federal law.

The National Center for Natural Products Research in Oxford, Mississippi is the only facility in the United States that is federally licensed by the National Institute on Drug Abuse to cultivate cannabis for scientific research. The Center is part of the School of Pharmacy at the University of Mississippi.

## USAGE

Roger Roffman, a professor of social work at the University of Washington, asserted in July 2009 that "approximately 3.6 million Americans are daily or near daily users."[2] Peter Reuter, a professor at the School of Public Policy and the Department of Criminology at the University of Maryland, said that "experimenting with marijuana has long been a normal part of growing up in the U.S.; about half of the population born since 1960 has tried the drug by age 21."[2] A World Health Organization survey found that the United States is the world's leading per capita marijuana consumer.[3] The 2007 National Survey on Drug Use & Health prepared by the U.S. Department of Human Health and Services indicates that over 100 million U.S. citizens over the age of 12 have used marijuana.[4]

# MEDICAL CANNABIS

In the United States, it is important to differentiate between medical cannabis at the federal and at the state level. At the federal level, cannabis *per se* has been made criminal by implementation of the Controlled Substances Act.

The Federal Food, Drug, and Cosmetic Act makes the U.S. Food and Drug Administration (FDA) the sole government entity responsible for ensuring the safety and efficacy of new prescription and over-the-counter drugs, overseeing the labeling and marketing of drugs, and regulating the manufacturing and packaging of drugs.[5] The FDA defines a drug as safe and effective for a specific indication if the clinical benefits to the patient are felt to outweigh any health risks the drug might pose. The FDA and comparable authorities in Western Europe including the Netherlands, have not approved *smoked* marijuana (some because of the problems related to smoking *per se*) for any condition or disease.[6][7] Cannabis remains illegal throughout the United States and is not approved for prescription as medicine, although 13 states - Alaska, California, Colorado, Hawaii, Maine, Michigan, Montana, Nevada, New Mexico, Oregon, Rhode Island, Vermont, and Washington - approve and regulate its medical use. A bill currently in the New Jersey senate would legalize medical use of marijuana if it passes. The federal government continues to enforce its prohibition in these states. However, there are also 3 states, Arizona, Massachusetts, and Maryland, whose drug laws are favorable towards the medicinal use of marijuana, in the latter case making it a non-incarcerable offense with a maximum penalty of a $100 fine,[1] but which still explicitly ban it. Most recently, in the 2008 election Michigan passed a referendum permitting the use of marijuana for medical purposes.

Potential health benefits aside, marijuana remains a U.S. federally controlled substance, making possession and distribution illegal. It has been estimated that an average marijuana clinic distributes a pound of cannabis per day, making acquisition a critical challenge. This acquisition may have to resort to more traditionally crime-associated, black-market sources, contributing to crime in communities. This point was illustrated in early 2007, with the murder of Denver, Colorado area medical cannabis activist Ken Gorman.[8]

Researchers face similar challenges in obtaining medical cannabis for research trial. Recently, the FDA has approved a number of cannabis research clinical trials, but the Drug Enforcement Agency has not granted licenses to the researchers in these studies.

Cannabis was listed in the United States Pharmacopeia from 1850 until 1942.[9] The United States federal government does not currently recognize any legitimate medical use, although there are currently five patients receiving cannabis for their various illnesses through the Compassionate Investigational New Drug program that was closed to new patients in 1991 by the George H. W. Bush administration. Francis L. Young, an administrative law judge with the United States Drug Enforcement Agency, in 1988, declared that "in its natural form, [cannabis] is one of the safest therapeutically active substances known."[10] However, smoked cannabis is today not approved by the United States Food and Drug Administration (FDA).[11] Thirteen U.S. state laws currently allow for the medicinal use of cannabis,[12] but the United States Supreme Court ruled that the federal government has the right to regulate and criminalize marijuana also in these states, even for medical purposes.

The term "medical marijuana" post-dates the U.S. Marijuana Tax Act of 1937, enacted by the Franklin D. Roosevelt administration, the effect of which made cannabis prescriptions illegal in the United States.

*I am going to accept a new job. I know I will have to do a drug screen which is fine and I*

*am not worried about passing it, but... will my
employer know what I am taking. I will disclose
the information at my screening but do they pass
this information on to my employer or do they
just let them know that I passed?*

*I don't have an exact answer for you because
it depends on your particular employer. But,
in a general sense, yes, the information most
often does get back to the employer. Maybe
not to the hiring manager per se, but to human
resources department. Most employment offers are
contingent on "passing the urine screen and / or
physical."*

*I don't mean to be vague, but a lot of it will
depend on what type of work you'll be doing, skill
set required, and etc. For example, if you were
a driver, no way would they employ you. Same
goes if you worked in a factory or some type of
production. Most companies won't even let you on
the property.*

*However, for more "white collar" or administrative
jobs, they may allow some things. A lot will
depend on how much they find, and how much
you tell them you take, why you take it, and etc.
Depending on what med it is and how much, they*

*may request a statement or some type of discussion
with your prescribing doctor. So, you may want
to give him a heads up. I don't mean to scare
you, but if they think your condition is "chronic"
and you're taking regular pain medications, they
may not hire you. They may also do more digging
as to why you are leaving your old job. In other
words, are you leaving because either your current
employer knows about the medications, or do
the medications cause secondary type issues...
Missing work, performance, and etc.?*

## Alaska

The medical use of cannabis was endorsed by 58%
of voters in Alaska in November 1998 and the law
became effective on March 4, 1999. The law legalizes
the possession, cultivation and use of cannabis for
patients who have received a certificate from a doctor
confirming they can benefit from the medical use
of cannabis. The conditions and symptoms eligible
are: cachexia, cancer, chronic pain, epilepsy and
other conditions characterized by spasms, chronic
glaucoma, HIV or AIDS, multiple sclerosis and nausea.
The state maintains a confidential list of patients who
are assigned an identity card.[13]

## California

Information about medical cannabis in the U.S. western state of California can be found here:[2] In 1996 California voted Proposition 215, also called the Compassionate Use Act, into law. CA Senate Bill 420 was passed in 2003 to clarify Proposition 215 by specifying statewide minimum limits on possession of marijuana and enact a Statewide Medical Marijuana ID Card Program (the G214 card). As of January 16, 2008, only 36 of 58 counties are issuing cards in the program, with 18,847 cards having been issued,[14] however, participation in the ID Card program is optional and the identification card is not required to claim the Act's protections.[15]

On November 5, 1996 56% of voters approved Proposition 215. The law removes state-level criminal penalties on the use, possession and cultivation of marijuana by patients who possess a "written or oral recommendation" from their physician that he or she "would benefit from medical marijuana." Patients diagnosed with any illness where the medical use of marijuana has been "deemed appropriate and has been recommended by a physician" are provided with legal protection under this act. Conditions typically covered by the law include: *arthritis; cachexia; cancer; chronic pain; HIV or AIDS; epilepsy; migraine; and multiple sclerosis*, with other less debilitating conditions like insomnia, reduced appetite, anxiety, and PTSD often treated also. No regulations regarding the amount of marijuana patients may possess and/or cultivate were provided by this act, though the California Legislature adopted guidelines in 2003.[16]

In 2009, California Assembly Bill 390 was introduced. If passed, it would legalize the sale of marijuana to those twenty-one and older.

## Oregon

Information about medical cannabis in the U.S. western state of Oregon can be found here:[7] The Oregon medical cannabis program has the name, "The Oregon Medical Marijuana Program," which administers the Medical Marijuana Act approved there by the public in November 1998.[20] The Oregon Medical Marijuana Program administers the program within the Oregon Department of Human Services. As of April 1, 2008, there were 16,635 patients registered.[21] Virtually all patients benefiting from the program suffer from severe pain and almost 2500 from nausea. The other conditions are given as epilepsy, AIDS / HIV, cancer, cachexia, chronic glaucoma and tremors caused by Alzheimer's disease.[22]

## Washington

The State of Washington adopted a law via elections in November 1998 (Initiative 692), legalizing the use, possession and cultivation of cannabis for patients with a medical certificate. The conditions are eligible the following: cachexia, cancer, HIV or AIDS, epilepsy, glaucoma, chronic pain otherwise intractable, and multiple sclerosis. According to the law in Washington,[10] a patient prescribed medical marijuana may only keep a 60 day supply of it.[24]

# LEGALITY

The Federal government has criminalized marijuana under the Interstate Commerce Clause, which gives the Federal Government the power to regulate the channels of commerce, the instrumentalities of commerce, and actions that substantially affect interstate commerce. Additionally, under the Supremacy Clause, any state law in conflict with federal law is not valid. These issues were addressed squarely by the United States Supreme Court in *Gonzales v. Raich*, 352 F. 3d 1222 in 2005. Twelve US states had passed laws allowing some degree of medical use (9 of the 12 by majority vote of the citizenry), while a further six states had taken steps to decriminalize it to some degree. This movement sought to make simple possession of cannabis punishable by only confiscation or a fine, rather than prison. In the past several years, the movement had started to have some successes. These included Denver, Colorado legalizing possession of up to an ounce of cannabis for adults aged 21 and older, though this age restriction has been criticized as age discrimination, since adults under 21 cannot legally possess it.[25]

In Alaska, cannabis was decidedly legal (under state, but not federal, law) for in-home, personal use under the *Ravin vs. State* ruling of 1975. This ruling allowed up to two ounces of cannabis and cultivation of fewer than 25 plants for these purposes. A 1991 voter ballot initiative recriminalized marijuana possession, but when that law was eventually challenged in 2004, the Alaska courts upheld the *Ravin* ruling, saying the popular vote could not trump the state constitution. In response to former Governor Frank Murkowski's successive attempt to re-criminalize cannabis, the American Civil Liberties Union (ACLU) filed a lawsuit against the state. On July 17, 2006, Superior Court Judge Patricia Collins awarded the Case Summary judgment to the ACLU. In her ruling, she said "No specific argument has been advanced in this case that possession of more than 1 ounce of cannabis, even within the privacy of the home, is constitutionally protected conduct under Ravin or that any plaintiff or ACLU of Alaska member actually possesses more than 1 ounce of cannabis in their homes." This does not mean that the legal possession threshold has been reduced to one ounce, as this was a mere case summary review filed by the ACLU, not a full case. Reinforcing *Ravin,* Collins wrote "A lower court cannot reverse the State Supreme Court's 1975 decision in Ravin v. State" and "Unless and until the Supreme Court directs otherwise, *Ravin* is the law in this state and this court is duty bound to follow that law". The law regarding possession of cannabis has not changed in Alaska, and the Supreme Court has declined to review the case, therefore the law still stands at four ounces. However, federal prosecutions under the CSA can be brought in Federal Court, and federal courts applying federal law are not bound by state court precedent. As such, federal courts in Alaska will recognize that possession of any quantity of marijuana remains illegal in Alaska under federal law.

In 2002, Nevada voters defeated a ballot question which would legalize up to three ounces for adults 21 and older by 39% to 61%. In 2006, a similar Nevada ballot initiative, which would have legalized and regulated the cultivation, distribution, and possession of up to 1 ounce of marijuana by adults 21 and older, was defeated by 44% to 56%.

In 2006, South Dakota voters defeated Measure 4, voting 48% for and 52% against. Measure 4 was to allow the use of medical marijuana by patients deemed by their physicians to benefit from its use, and was to be regulated by state-issued ID cards and protection of legitimate medical distributors.

In 2008, Massachusetts voters approved a ballot initiative to decriminalize a possession of up to an ounce of marijuana.[26]

In the November election of 2008, Michigan became the thirteenth state to legalize the physician supervised possession and use of cannabis. More than 60 percent of Michigan voters decided in favor of Proposal 1, which establishes a state-regulated system regarding the use and cultivation of medical marijuana by qualified patients.

In January 2009, President Barack Obama's transition team organized a poll to clarify some of the top issues the American public wants to have his administration look into, and two of the top ten ideas were to legalize the use of cannabis.[27]

# CRIME

There have been over eight million cannabis arrests in the United States since 1993, including 786,545 arrests in 2005. Cannabis users have been arrested at the rate of 1 every 40 seconds. About 88% of all marijuana arrests are for possession - not manufacture or distribution.[28]

Although large-scale marijuana growing operations are frequently targeted by police in raids to attack the supply side and discourage the spread and marketing of the drug, the great majority of those arrested for cannabis are there for possession alone.[29] However, in 1997, the vast majority of inmates in state prisons for marijuana related convictions were convicted of offenses other than simple possession.[30]

Marijuana arrests for the year 2007 were recorded at 872,721. This tops 2006's record high by five percent.[31]

# POLITICAL PARTIES

In the United States there is the United States Marijuana Party that has local chapters in 29 states. There are also state-level parties. Members associated with the US Marijuana Party have run for office, including Edward Forchion (for multiple offices) and candidates from the Marijuana Reform Party (for governor).

• Minnesota has the Grassroots Party.

• In New Jersey there is The Legalize Marijuana Party founded by Manee Kassaii on April 20, 1998.

• In New York State, in 1998 and 2002, the Marijuana Reform Party of New York State ran candidates for governor and other statewide offices. In 2004, a federal judge held that, by running candidates in 1998 and 2002 statewide elections, the Marijuana Reform Party demonstrated a "modicum of support" sufficient to entitle it to an injunction compelling the state board of elections to recognize the party and allow voters to enroll in it. Viable in New York State because of its unique fusion political system, it remains the only political party in the United States recognized on a statewide level and dedicated to the advocacy of marijuana law reform, with the exception of the Libertarian Party, which advocates legalization of all drugs.

• In the State of Vermont, Cris Ericson was on the official election ballot in 2004 for the Marijuana Party for Governor and for U.S. Senate. It is legal to be on the official election ballot for one state and one federal office. Cris Ericson will be on the official election ballot 2008 for U.S. Congress House of Representatives and for Governor of Vermont for the U.S. Marijuana Party. http://makemarijuanalegal.com

## Notable Pro-Medical Cannabis Individuals

Supporters of legalizing cannabis for medical use range from actors and musicians to politicians, writers, and scientists. Major activists include Steve Kubby, Ethan Nadelmann, Dennis Peron, Angel Raich, Robert Randall,[164] Keith Stroup, and Marc Emery.

Politicians from multiple parties support medicinal marijuana use[165] Democratic members of Congress Barney Frank, Dennis Kucinich, and Sam Farr, Republican Congress members Ron Paul,[166] and Dana Rohrabacher, the late Republican State Senator Bill Mescher, and Libertarian Loretta Nall.

Researchers and scientist advocates include Jay Cavanaugh, PhD, Lyle Craker, PhD, Milton Friedman,

PhD, Stephen Jay Gould, Lester Grinspoon, MD, Bob Melamede, PhD[167] and Carl Sagan, PhD.

Writers, such as the late William F. Buckley, Fred Gardner, Christopher Hitchens,[168] Jack Herer, Peter McWilliams, Salman Rushdie, Ann Druyan, Ed Rosenthal, Rick Steves, Samuel Thompson, and Robert Anton Wilson also support the legalization of medical cannabis.

## Notable Anti-Medical Cannabis Individuals

Politicians that oppose the medicinal use of cannabis include former Drug Czars Andrea Barthwell, William Bennett,[169] Barry McCaffrey,[170] and John P. Walters, former U.S. Presidents George H. W. Bush, Bill Clinton and George W. Bush, congressmen Theodore Sophocleus[171] and Mark Souder, and former governors Mitt Romney[172] and Eliot Spitzer.

Attorney Generals Michael Mukasey, Janet Reno, and Dan Lungren also prefer cannabis to be illegal, as well as former U.S. Prosecutors Bonnie Dumanis,[173] Carol Lam, and Asa Hutchinson,[174] former Surgeon General Richard Carmona,[175] former Solicitor General Paul Clement, International Narcotics Control Board president Hamid Ghodse, Republican Senior Senator John McCain,[176] and former U.S. Secretary of Health and Human Services Donna Shalala. Conservative talk show hosts, such Rush Limbaugh[177] and Hal Lindsey, also oppose the use of medical cannabis.

# LEGAL AND MEDICAL STATUS OF CANNABIS IN THE US

European laws on cannabis possession (small amount). Data are from multiple sources detailed on the full source list

As a Schedule I drug under the federal Controlled Substances Act of 1970, marijuana (cannabis) is considered to have "no accepted medical use" and is illegal for any reason, with the exception of FDA-approved research programs. The Act allows mis-controlled substances to be reclassified by petition by any member of the public, but federal agencies have so far denied each such petition on behalf of cannabis. (See removal of cannabis from Schedule I of the Controlled Substances Act.)

A successful "medical necessity" defense by patient Robert Randall led the FDA to create an "Investigational New Drug Program", which provides medical cannabis grown under a NIDA contract at the Research Institute for Pharmaceutical Science at the University of Mississippi to a small number of patients since 1978. The program was closed to new patients in 1992 when many AIDS patients applied.

Six living patients continue to receive federal marijuana, including, since 1983, Irvin Rosenfeld[2]

(for bone spurs), a 52-year-old stockbroker who has been featured in numerous print articles and on the *Penn & Teller: Bullshit!* cable television series; Elvy Musikka (for glaucoma); and George McMahon (who authored[3] Prescription Pot), a book detailing the federal program, which contains the only existing medical study performed on the legal patients. The marijuana is grown on a farm at the University of Mississippi in Oxford and each person receives 300 joints a month. These patients are required by the U. S. Government to smoke the marijuana through a "rolled paper tube" (they are not allowed to eat it or use pipes or vaporizers). Patients and their doctors report significant medical benefits from their use of marijuana.

There is a split between the U. S. federal and many state governments over medical marijuana policy. On June 6, 2005, the Supreme Court, in *Gonzales v. Raich,* ruled in a 6-3 decision that Congress has the right to outlaw medicinal cannabis, thus subjecting all patients to federal prosecution even in states where the treatment is legalized. Currently, there are at least thirteen states with effective medical marijuana laws on the books: Alaska, California, Colorado, Hawaii, Maine, Michigan, Montana, Nevada, New Mexico, Oregon, Rhode Island, Vermont, and

Washington. Maryland's law does not legalize
possession of medical cannabis, but rather makes it a
non-incarcerable offense with a maximum penalty of
a $100 fine.[5]

The case brought into tension two themes of the
Rehnquist court: the limits it has imposed on the
federal government and the latitude it has afforded
law enforcement officers. Those issues produced an
unusual breakdown among the nine justices.

Joining Justice John Paul Stevens's majority decision
were Justices Anthony M. Kennedy, David H. Souter,
Ruth Bader Ginsburg and Stephen G. Breyer. Justice
Antonin Scalia wrote separately to say he agreed with
the result, though not the majority's reasoning. Chief
Justice William H. Rehnquist and Justices Sandra Day
O'Connor and Clarence Thomas dissented.

DEA and NIDA opposition prevented any scientific
studies of medical marijuana for more than a decade,
but in the 1990s, activists and doctors were energized
by seeing marijuana help dying AIDS patients. A study
of smoked marijuana at the University of California,
San Francisco, under Dr. Donald Abrams was
approved after five years. Further research followed,
particularly due to a ten million dollar research
appropriation by the California legislature. The

University of California coordinates this research.[6] However, there are still significant barriers, unique among Schedule I substances, to conducting medical marijuana research in the US.[4] Many years of work remain before sufficient research could be approved and conducted to meet the FDA's standards for approving marijuana as a new prescription medicine.

Public opinion surveys find most Americans support legalization of medical marijuana, even as they reject broader legalization of the drug. A November 2003 Gallup survey found 75% said they would favor use of marijuana under a doctor's prescription, but nearly two-thirds rejected full legalization.[7][8] While Congress has consistently rejected legislation to allow medical use of marijuana, 33 states and the District of Columbia have authorized it in some form.[9] Most require that it be "prescribed", which is problematic when federal agencies control doctors' power to prescribe. Twelve states have made laws which permit doctors to instead "recommend" marijuana, starting with California Proposition 215 (1996). The most recent such state was Rhode Island on January 3, 2006, when its state legislature overturned a gubernatorial veto of a bill legalizing medical marijuana. In 2004, Montana legalized medical marijuana by a statewide referendum.

Hawaii, Maine and Maryland have legalized medical marijuana by legislative action, and the California legislature expanded patient protections in 2003. District of Columbia voters also passed several medical marijuana initiatives, but Congress first denied the funds to count the vote, then when that was declared unconstitutional, voted to overturn the initiative. Even in these states, law enforcement agencies and individual officers sometimes continue to arrest users. For example, the official position of the California Narcotics Officers Association is that medical marijuana activists "misled" the public which voted to change the law.[10] Legal and social support groups such as Americans for Safe Access [11] have sprung up in defense.

Sale of medical marijuana is illegal or barely legal, even in states where patients have the right to grow or use it, due to public confusion between dispensaries and "drug dealers". However, medical marijuana dispensaries have been established in many locations, particularly in California, where they work openly with local government officials to resolve any difficulties. Many offer social services, medical consultations, and support groups as well as medicine. The first such dispensary, known as the Cannabis Buyers Club (CBC), was opened by Dennis

Peron in February, 1994. The club operated openly
in San Francisco for years, even before medical
marijuana was legalized. Local police and politicians
did not want to be seen arresting suffering AIDS
patients, or denying them any medicine that could
help them. This gay community activism led directly
to the "Compassionate Use Act" medical marijuana
initiative, California Proposition 215 (1996), which
voters approved.

Washington state Initiative 692, passed by the
voters in 1998, also authorizes the medical use of
marijuana. On November 2 2004, the voters of Ann
Arbor, Michigan passed a similar resolution with 74%
approval. In early 2005, Rhode Island's legislature was
the first to legalize medical marijuana. Such an act
was not sent to the voters.

In NYC, in 2001, well known local activist Kenny
Toglia, known by some as "The Dog," achieved
a significant victory for medical cannabis when
charges against him were dropped in the infamous
"marijuana cookie case". Kenny Toglia in 2001 was
involved in a historic drug policy case involving
medical marijuana in NYS. He was arrested at
"University of the Streets", a locally owned black
community center on the corner of Tompkins
Square at East 7th Street, with more than a pound of

marijuana. Ultimately, all charges against him were dismissed following his complaint that the arresting officers had consumed a number of oatmeal cookies laced with marijuana which had been intended for use by patients with AIDS suffering from wasting syndrome. The events following his arrest led to the issue becoming important in the NYS gubernatorial campaign, and subsequently turned the statewide political tide in favor of the issue.[12]

Although the DEA states that they "don't target sick and dying people",[13] federal arrests of medical marijuana users and suppliers continue. Close to thirty federal criminal cases about medical marijuana are pending. Several jurisdictions, including Oakland, California and San Mateo County, California have announced plans to distribute medical marijuana to patients. Ed Rosenthal, author of dozens of books on marijuana cultivation, grew small "starter" plants for patients on behalf of the city government of Oakland. He was convicted in federal court of manufacturing marijuana, by a jury which was never told that his marijuana was for medical patients. Shortly after the trial, eight of the fourteen jurors (and alternates) who convicted him called a press conference and denounced their verdict, arguing that the trial was not fair because the evidence that Rosenthal was growing marijuana for medical use, working on behalf of the city, and was told by DEA agents and city officials that he was immune to prosecution, was all suppressed by the judge as "irrelevant under federal law". The jury discovered the real facts by reading newspapers, within hours after delivering their verdict. As a result of the intense public scrutiny, Rosenthal was given the most lenient possible sentence - only one day - since they had already found him guilty and could not change their verdict. He is appealing his felony conviction, and the federal government is appealing the short sentence.

The late Peter McWilliams, a vocal supporter of medical cannabis who is terminally ill with AIDS and cancer, was arrested by the DEA and convicted for violating federal marijuana laws. Even as he vomited repeatedly during court proceedings, McWilliams was not allowed by the federal judge to explain his condition or its connection to the charges against him. His mother's house had been used to collateralize the bond on which he was allowed to remain free pending sentencing, a condition of which was that he refrain from using cannabis. Prior to his death, McWilliams stated

*The federal prosecutor personally called my mother to tell her that if I was found with even a trace of medical marijuana, her house would be taken away.*[14]

Richard Cowan and many other critics of U. S. drug policies have described his death as murder by the federal government, insofar as they denied him the use of the medical cannabis which might have prevented his death.

The federal government of the United States continues to argue that smoked cannabis has no recognized medical purpose (pointing to a definition of "medical purpose" published by the DEA, not the Food and Drug Administration, the National Institutes of Health, the Centers for Disease Control, or the office of the U. S. Surgeon General and the U. S. Public Health Service) -- many officials point to the difficulty of regulating dosage (a problem for treatment as well as research) despite the availability (in Canada and the U. K.) of dosage-controlled Sativex. The United States has also pressured other governments (especially Canada, with which it shares a largely open border) to retain restrictions on marijuana.

The most recently added state to those with decriminalization status is Massachusetts. On November 4, 2008, Massachusetts Ballot question #2 passed. This question was for the decriminalization of possession of an ounce or less for personal use. In Massachusetts, it passed at almost a 2:1 ratio.

# REFERENCES – MEDICAL CANNABIS

1. "Cannabis sativa information from NPGS/GRIN". www.ars-grin.gov. http://www.amjbot.org/cgi/content/abstract/91/6/966. Retrieved on 2008-07-13.

2. "Marijuana and Medicine: Assessing the Science Base". Nap.edu. http://www.nap.edu/openbook.php?record_id=6376&page=13. Retrieved on 2009-04-26.

3. "NIH Workshop on the Medical Utility of Marijuana - Part 1". Medmjscience.org. http://www.medmjscience.org/Pages/reports/nihpt1.html. Retrieved on 2009-04-26.

4. "CannabisMD Reports : Marijuana in Capsules". Cannabismd.org. http://cannabismd.org/reports/mjcapsules.php. Retrieved on 2009-04-26.

5. "Methods of ingestion | Michigan Medical Marijuana Association | News and Information for Michigan's medical marijuana patients and caregivers". Michiganmedicalmarijuana.org. http://michiganmedicalmarijuana.org/node/1030. Retrieved on 2009-04-26.

6. 13 Legal Medical Marijuana States: Laws, Fees, and Possession Limits", ProCon.org. Retrieved April 21, 2009.

7. "Portugal's drug decriminalization 'bizarrely underappreciated': Greenwald". The Raw Story. 2009-04-06. http://rawstory.com/news/2008/Portugals_drug_decriminalization_bizarrely_underappreciated_Greenwald_0406.html. Retrieved on 2009-04-26.

8. http://www.myfoxcharlotte.com/myfox/pages/Home/Detail?contentId=8453681&version=1&locale=EN-US&layoutCode=TSTY&pageId=1.1.1

9. http://www.mpp.org/states/new-york/news/approval-predicted-for.html

10. "Cannabinoids as antioxidants and neuroprotectants - US Patent 6630507 Abstract". Patentstorm.us. http://www.patentstorm.us/patents/6630507.html. Retrieved on 2009-04-26.

11. "Inter-Agency Advisory Regarding Claims That Smoked Marijuana Is a Medicine". Fda.gov. 2006-04-20. http://www.fda.gov/bbs/topics/NEWS/2006/NEW01362.html. Retrieved on 2009-04-26.

12. http://www.wamm.org/

13. http://www.canorml.org/prop/Mikuriya_ICD-9list.pdf

14. Dale Gieringer, "Medical Use of Cannabis in California," in Franjo Grotenhermen, M.D. & Ethan Russo, M.D., ed., Cannabis and Cannabinoids: Pharmacology, Toxicology and Therapeutic Potential, Haworth Press, 2002 [1]

15. Grotenhermen, Franjo (2002). *Cannabis and Cannabinoids*. New York: Haworth Integrative Healing Press. p. 124. ISBN 9780789015082.

16. Cannabis-based drugs could offer new hope for [inflammatory bowel disease patients]

17. http://www.freedomtoexhale.com/clinical.pdf

18. http://www.cmcr.ucsd.edu/geninfo/CannabinoidsMS_Lancet11-03.pdf

19. http://www.medicalmarijuanainformation.com/therapeuticuses/patientGroups.php?groupID=19

20. http://www.ncbi.nlm.nih.gov/pubmed/2175265?dopt=Abstract

21. http://www.ncbi.nlm.nih.gov/pubmed/11854790?dopt=Abstract

22. http://www.ncbi.nlm.nih.gov/pubmed/6978699?dopt=Abstract

23. http://www.doctordeluca.com/Library/WOD/WPS3-MedMj/CannabinoidsMedMetaAnalysis06.pdf

24. "Machinery Of The 'Marijuana Munchies'". Sciencedaily.com. 2005-12-26. http://www.sciencedaily.com/releases/2005/12/051226102503.htm. Retrieved on 2009-04-26.

25. "Role of cannabinoid receptors in alcohol abuse, study". Medicalnewstoday.com. http://www.medicalnewstoday.com/articles/30338.php. Retrieved on 2009-04-26.

26. http://video.google.com/videoplay?docid=-1820696077430281885

27. Beaucar, Kelley (2004-04-20). "Cannabis 'Scrips to Calm Kids? - Politics | Republican Party | Democratic Party | Political Spectrum". FOXNews.com. http://www.foxnews.com/story/0,2933,117541,00.html. Retrieved on 2009-04-26.

28. http://ajh.sagepub.com/cgi/content/abstract/18/4/264

29. David Kohn, Baltimore Sun (2004-11-05). "Researchers buzzing about marijuana-derived medicines / Cannabinoids may help against many diseases". Sfgate.com. http://www.sfgate.com/cgi-bin/article.cgi?file=/chronicle/archive/2004/11/05/MNGV39LE091.DTL&type=printable. Retrieved on 2009-04-26.

30. http://www.ncbi.nlm.nih.gov/sites/entrez?cmd=Retrieve&db=PubMed&dopt=Abstract&list_uids=16183560

31. "The nonpsychoactive cannabis constituent cannabidiol is an oral anti-arthritic therapeutic in murine collagen-induced arthritis — PNAS". Pnas.org. 2000-08-15. http://www.pnas.org/content/97/17/9561.full. Retrieved on 2009-04-26.

32. "Pot-Based Drug Promising for Arthritis". Webmd.com. http://www.webmd.com/rheumatoid-arthritis/news/20051108/pot-based-drug-promising-for-arthritis. Retrieved on 2009-04-26.

33. "Effects of Smoked Marijuana in Experimentally Induced Asthma". Druglibrary.org. http://www.druglibrary.org/schaffer/hemp/medical/tashkin/tashkin1.htm. Retrieved on 2009-04-26.

34. "Cannabis may help keep arteries clear - health - 16 April 2005". New Scientist. doi:10.1038/nature03389. http://www.newscientist.com/article/mg18624956.000. Retrieved on 2009-04-26.

35. "Prenatal Marijuana Exposure and Neonatal Outcomes in Jamaica: An Ethnographic Study". Druglibrary.org. http://www.druglibrary.org/schaffer/hemp/medical/can-babies.htm. Retrieved on 2009-04-26.

36. "The Use of Cannabis as a Mood Stabilizer in Bipolar Disorder". Ukcia.org. http://www.ukcia.org/research/TheUseofCannabisasaMoodStabilizerinBipolarDisorder.html. Retrieved on 2009-04-26.

37. http://www.ncbi.nlm.nih.gov/pubmed/15888515?dopt=Abstract&holding=f1000,f1000m,isrctn

38. "Recipe For Trouble". CBS News. 2007-01-15. http://www.cbsnews.com/stories/2002/03/05/48hours/main503022.shtml. Retrieved on 2009-04-26.

39. "Dr. Tod Mikuriya: Cannabis as a Frontline Treatment for Childhood Mental Disorders". Counterpunch.org. http://www.counterpunch.org/mikuriya07082006.html. Retrieved on 2009-04-26.

40. Home (2005-08-11). "The endogenous cannabinoid, anandamide, induces cell death in colorectal carcinoma cells: a possible role for cyclooxygenase 2 - Patsos et al. 54 (12): 1741 - Gut". Gut.bmj.com. doi:10.1136/gut.2005.073403. http://gut.bmj.com/cgi/content/abstract/54/12/1741. Retrieved on 2009-04-26.

41. "Marijuana Improves Depression in Low Doses, Worsens It in High Doses, Study Says - Health News | Current Health News | Medical News". FOXNews.com. 2007-10-25. http://www.foxnews.com/story/0,2933,304996,00.html. Retrieved on 2009-04-26.

42. http://www.doctordeluca.com/Library/WOD/WPS3-MedMj/DecreasedDepressionInMjUsers05.pdf

43. "Journal of Clinical Investigation - Cannabinoids promote embryonic and adult hippocampus neurogenesis and produce anxiolytic- and antidepressant-like effects". Jci.org. http://www.jci.org/articles/view/25509/version/1. Retrieved on 2009-04-26.

44. "AAMC: Cannabis and Depression". Pacifier.com. http://www.pacifier.com/~alive/cmu/depression_and_cannabis.htm. Retrieved on 2009-04-26.

45. "Marijuana Compound May Help Stop Diabetic Retinopathy". Sciencedaily.com. 2006-02-27. http://www.sciencedaily.com/releases/2006/02/060227184647.htm. Retrieved on 2009-04-26.

46. "Marijuana Compound May Help Stop Diabetic Retinopathy". Defeat Diabetes. 2006-03-17. http://www.defeatdiabetes.org/Articles/retinopathy_marijuana060317.htm. Retrieved on 2009-04-26.

**47.** "Neuroprotective and Blood-Retinal Barrier-Preserving Effects of Cannabidiol in Experimental Diabetes - El-Remessy *et al.* 168 (1): 235 - American Journal of Pathology". Ajp.amjpathol.org. doi:10.2353/ajpath.2006.050500. http://ajp. amjpathol.org/cgi/content/abstract/168/1/235. Retrieved on 2009-04-26.

**48.** "Dystonia". NORML. http://www.norml.org/index.cfm?Group_ID=7006. Retrieved on 2009-04-26.

**49.** http://www.ncbi.nlm.nih.gov/pubmed/11835452?dopt=Abstract

**50.** "Marijuana-Like Chemicals in the Brain Calm Neurons - MedPot.net/Forums". Medpot.net. http://www.medpot.net/forums/index.php?showtopic=9686. Retrieved on 2009-04-26.

**51.** "Gastrointestinal Disorders". NORML. http://www.norml.org/index. cfm?Group_ID=7009. Retrieved on 2009-04-26.

**52.** "Informa Pharmaceutical Science - Expert Opinion on Investigational Drugs - 12(1):39 - Summary". Informapharmascience.com. 2005-03-02. doi:10.1517/1 3543784.12.1.39. http://www.informapharmascience.com/doi/abs/10.1517/13 543784.12.1.39. Retrieved on 2009-04-26.

**53.** "Amphiregulin is a factor for resistance of glioma cells to cannabinoid-induced apoptosis". Marijuana.researchtoday.net. 2009-02-20. doi:10.1002/ glia.20856. http://marijuana.researchtoday.net/archive/6/2/2201.htm. Retrieved on 2009-04-26.

**54.** "Inhibition of Cancer Cell Invasion by Cannabinoids via Increased Expression of Tissue Inhibitor of Matrix Metalloproteinases-1 - Ramer and Hinz 100 (1): 59 - JNCI Journal of the National Cancer Institute". Jnci.oxfordjournals.org. doi:10.1093/jnci/djm268. http://jnci.oxfordjournals.org/cgi/reprint/100/1/59. Retrieved on 2009-04-26.

**55.** "Hepatitis C". NORML. http://www.norml.org/index.cfm?Group_ID=7010. Retrieved on 2009-04-26.

**56.** "European Journal of Gastroenterology & Hepatology". Journals.lww.com. doi:10.1097/01.meg.0000216934.22114.51. http://journals.lww.com/eurojgh/ pages/articleviewer.aspx?year=2006&issue=10000&article=00005&type=abstr act. Retrieved on 2009-04-26.

**57.** "Cannabidiol: The Wonder Drug of the 21st Century?". Druglibrary.org. http:// www.druglibrary.org/schaffer/hemp/medical/cannabid.htm. Retrieved on 2009-04-26.

**58.** "Lowering of Blood Pressure Through Use of Hashish: The Hempire - [cannabis, britain]". The Hempire. 2006-06-20. http://www.thehempire. com/index.php/cannabis/news/lowering_of_blood_pressure_through_use_of_ hashish. Retrieved on 2009-04-26.

59. "Blood Pressure Lowered With Cannabis Component: The Hempire - [cannabis, uk]". The Hempire. 2006-06-15. http://www.thehempire.com/index. php/cannabis/news/blood_pressure_lowered_with_cannabis_component. Retrieved on 2009-04-26.

60. "Incontinence". NORML. http://www.norml.org/index.cfm?Group_ID=7012. Retrieved on 2009-04-26.

61. "Blood - Cannabis-induced cytotoxicity in leukemic cell lines: the role of the cannab". Bloodjournal.hematologylibrary.org. doi:10.1182/blood-2004-03-1182. http://bloodjournal.hematologylibrary.org/cgi/content/abstract/105/3/1214. Retrieved on 2009-04-26.

62. "Peer-Reviewed Studies on Marijuana - Medical Marijuana - ProCon. org". Medicalmarijuana.procon.org. http://medicalmarijuana.procon.org/viewresource.asp?resourceID=000884. Retrieved on 2009-04-26.

63. "Journal of Clinical Investigation - Inhibition of skin tumor growth and angiogenesis in vivo by activation of cannabinoid receptors". Jci.org. 2003-01-01. doi:10.1038/sj.onc.1201928. http://www.jci.org/articles/view/16116/version/1. Retrieved on 2009-04-26.

64. http://74.6.239.67/search/cache?ei=UTF-8&p=Vancouver+Island+Compassion+Society%2C+morning+sickness%2C+marijuana&fr=slv8-msgr&u=www. mercycenters.org/libry/info_Mothers.doc&w=vancouver+island+compassion+society+societies+morning+sickness+marijuana&d=KJVscZ2uSZD2&icp=1&.intl=us

65. "Mothering Magazine Birth Preparation Article: Medical Marijuana for Severe Morning Sickness". Mothering.com. http://www.mothering.com/articles/pregnancy_birth/birth_preparation/marijuana.html. Retrieved on 2009-04-26.

66. "A New MRSA Defense". Technology Review. http://www.technologyreview. com/biomedicine/21366/. Retrieved on 2009-04-26.

67. "Marijuana Ingredients May Fight MRSA". Webmd.com. 2008-09-04. http://www.webmd.com/news/20080904/marijuana-chemicals-may-fight-mrsa. Retrieved on 2009-04-26.

68. "Chemicals in Marijuana May Fight MRSA - Infectious Diseases: Causes, Types, Prevention, Treatment and Facts on". Medicinenet.com. 2008-09-04. http://www.medicinenet.com/script/main/art.asp?articlekey=92425. Retrieved on 2009-04-26.

69. "Enhancing activity of marijuana-like chemicals in brain helps treat Parkinson's symptoms in mice, Stanford study finds - Office of Communications & Public Affairs - Stanford University School of Medicine". Med.stanford.edu. http://med.stanford.edu/news_releases/2007/february/malenka.html. Retrieved on 2009-04-26.

70. Michael Hess (2005-12-11). "Science: Cream with endocannabinoids effective in the treatment of pruritus due to kidney disease". BBSNews. http://bbsnews.net/article.php/20051211212223236. Retrieved on 2009-04-26.

71. "Journal of Hepatology : The pruritus of cholestasis". ScienceDirect. 2005-10-06. doi:10.1016/j.jhep.2005.09.004. http://www.sciencedirect.com/science?_ob=ArticleURL&_udi=B6W7C-4H8FTRF-2&_user=10&_rdoc=1&_fmt=&_orig=search&_sort=d&view=c&_acct=C000050221&_version=1&_urlVersion=0&_userid=10&md5=b5834b8cb12cdee2e01a3910314feb79. Retrieved on 2009-04-26.

72. "Natural high helps banish bad memories - 31 July 2002". New Scientist. http://www.newscientist.com/article/dn2616-natural-high-helps-banish-bad-memories.html. Retrieved on 2009-04-26.

73. "Medical Marijuana: PTSD Medical Malpractice". Salem-News.Com. http://salem-news.com/articles/june142007/leveque_61407.php. Retrieved on 2009-04-26.

74. "IACM-Bulletin". Cannabis-med.org. http://www.cannabis-med.org/english/bulletin/ww_en_db_cannabis_artikel.php?id=123#1. Retrieved on 2009-04-26.

75. "AAMC: Those who suffer from sickle-cell disease experience painful episodes or attacks". Pacifier.com. http://www.pacifier.com/~alive/cmu/Sickle_cell.htm. Retrieved on 2009-04-26.

76. "Pot Constituents Dramatically Reduce Sleep Apnea, Study Says". NORML. http://norml.org/index.cfm?Group_ID=5323. Retrieved on 2009-04-26.

77. http://www.ncbi.nlm.nih.gov/pubmed/12071539?dopt=Abstract

78. "The Scripps Research Institute". Scripps.edu. 2006-08-09. http://www.scripps.edu/news/press/080906.html. Retrieved on 2009-04-26.

79. 7:10 p.m. ET (2006-10-10). "Marijuana may help stave off Alzheimer's - Alzheimer's Disease- msnbc.com". MSNBC. http://www.msnbc.msn.com/id/15145917/. Retrieved on 2009-04-26.

80. "Study Shows Marijuana Promotes Neuron Growth - OhmyNews International". English.ohmynews.com. 2005-10-17. http://english.ohmynews.com/articleview/article_view.asp?menu=c10400&no=253377&rel_no=1. Retrieved on 2009-04-26.

81. "Marijuana Cuts Lung Cancer Tumor Growth In Half, Study Shows". Sciencedaily.com. 2007-04-17. http://www.sciencedaily.com/releases/2007/04/070417193338.htm. Retrieved on 2009-04-26.

82. "Pot Smoking Not Linked to Lung Cancer". Webmd.com. 2006-05-23. http://www.webmd.com/lung-cancer/news/20060523/pot-smoking-not-linked-to-lung-cancer. Retrieved on 2009-04-26.

83. "Study Finds No Cancer-Marijuana Connection". washingtonpost.com. http://www.washingtonpost.com/wp-dyn/content/article/2006/05/25/AR2006052501729.html?referrer=digg. Retrieved on 2009-04-26.

84. "Medical News: ATS: Marijuana Smoking Found Non-Carcinogenic - in Hematology/Oncology, Lung Cancer from". MedPage Today. 2006-05-24. http://www.medpagetoday.com/HematologyOncology/LungCancer/3393. Retrieved on 2009-04-26.

85. "Marijuana smoking increases risk of COPD for tobacco smokers". Physorg.com. 2009-04-13. http://www.physorg.com/news158861123.html. Retrieved on 2009-04-26.

86. [2][dead link]

87. [3]

88. "Marijuana Compound May Stop Breast Cancer From Spreading, Study Says - Health News | Current Health News | Medical News". FOXNews.com. 2007-11-19. http://www.foxnews.com/story/0,2933,312132,00.html. Retrieved on 2009-04-26.

89. cc (2007-11-01). "Sean D. McAllister, PhD-Research in treament of aggressive breast cancers". Cpmc.org. http://www.cpmc.org/professionals/research/programs/science/sean.html. Retrieved on 2009-04-26.

90. (2007-11-20). "Cannabis compound may stop breast cancer spreading". News-medical.net. http://www.news-medical.net/?id=32724. Retrieved on 2009-04-26.

91. "Human Immunodeficiency Virus (HIV)". NORML. http://www.norml.org/index.cfm?Group_ID=7485#10. Retrieved on 2009-04-26.

92. "Short-Term Effects of Cannabinoids in Patients with HIV-1 Infection: A Randomized, Placebo-Controlled Clinical Trial - Abrams et al. 139 (4): 258 - Annals of Internal Medicine". Annals.org. 2003-08-19. http://www.annals.org/cgi/content/abstract/139/4/258. Retrieved on 2009-04-26.

93. "Marijuana Eases Nerve Pain Due to HIV". Webmd.com. 2008-08-06. http://www.webmd.com/hiv-aids/news/20080805/marijuana-eases-nerve-pain-due-to-hiv. Retrieved on 2009-04-26.

94. "News Research Updates July-August 2008". Pain-topics.org. http://pain-topics.org/news_research_updates/issue16.php#Pot. Retrieved on 2009-04-26.

95. "Cannabis in painful HIV-associated sensory neuropathy: A randomized placebo-controlled trial - Abrams et al. 68 (7): 515". Neurology. doi:10.1212/01.wnl.0000253187.66183.9c. http://www.neurology.org/cgi/content/abstract/68/7/515. Retrieved on 2009-04-26.

96. "Active Ingredient in Marijuana Kills Brain Cancer Cells". Forbes.com. http://www.forbes.com/feeds/hscout/2009/04/01/hscout625697.html. Retrieved on 2009-04-26.

97. "Marijuana Chemical May Fight Brain Cancer". CBS News. 2009-04-04. http://www.cbsnews.com/stories/2009/04/02/health/webmd/main4913095.shtml?source=RSSattr=Health_4913095. Retrieved on 2009-04-26.

**98.** "Journal of Clinical Investigation - Cannabinoid action induces autophagy-mediated cell death through stimulation of ER stress in human glioma cells". Jci.org. 2009-04-01. doi:10.1172/JCI37948DS1. http://www.jci.org/articles/view/37948. Retrieved on 2009-04-26.

**99.** http://www.ncbi.nlm.nih.gov/pubmed/11586361

**100.** http://www.nature.com/npp/journal/vaop/ncurrent/abs/npp200970a.html

**101.** http://www.redorbit.com/news/health/1716066/the_surprising_effect_of_marijuana_on_morphine_dependence/

**102.** http://www.physorg.com/news166196260.html

**103.** http://www.ncbi.nlm.nih.gov/pubmed/19444734?dopt=Abstract

**104.** http://www.mikuriya.com/cw_depend.html

**105.** http://www.pubmedcentral.nih.gov/picrender.fcgi?artid=1503422&blobtype=pdf

**106.** Grlie, L (1976). "A comparative study on some chemical and biological characteristics of various samples of cannabis resin". *Bulletin on Narcotics* **14:** 37–46.

**107.** Mechoulam R, Peters M, Murillo-Rodriguez E, Hanus LO (August 2007). "Cannabidiol - recent advances". *Chemistry & Biodiversity* **4** (8): 1678–1692. doi:10.1002/cbdv.200790147. PMID 17712814.

**108.** Zuardi, A.W; J.A.S. Crippa, J.E.C. Hallak, F.A. Moreira, F.S. Guimarães (2006). "Cannabidiol as an antipsychotic drug" (PDF). *Brazilian Journal of Medical and Biological Research* **39:** 421–429. ISSN 0100-879X ISSN 0100-879X. http://www.scielo.br/pdf/bjmbr/v39n4/6164.pdf.

**109.** McAllister SD, Christian RT, Horowitz MP, Garcia A, Desprez PY (2007). "Cannabidiol as a novel inhibitor of Id-1 gene expression in aggressive breast cancer cells". *Mol. Cancer Ther.* **6** (11): 2921–7. doi:10.1158/1535-7163.MCT-07-0371. PMID 18025276.

**110.** Article on BBC site

**111.** Cannabidiol and (–)Δ9-tetrahydrocannabinol are neuroprotective antioxidants, A. J. Hampson, M. Grimaldi, J. Axelrod, and D. Wink, Proc Natl Acad Sci U S A. 1998 July 7; 95(14): 8268–8273.

**112.** "Why Cannabis Stems Inflammation". www.sciencedaily.com. http://www.sciencedaily.com/releases/2008/07/080720222549.htm. Retrieved on 2008-08-21.

**113.** FDA Press Release

**114.** Koch, W. 23 Jun 2005. Spray alternative to pot on the market in Canada. *USA Today* (online). Retrieved on 27 February 2007

115. "Sativex - Investigational Cannabis-Based Treatment for Pain and Multiple Sclerosis Drug Development Technology". www.drugdevelopment-technology.com. http://www.drugdevelopment-technology.com/projects/sativex/. Retrieved on 2008-08-08.

116. "Europe: Sativex Coming to England, Spain". http://stopthedrugwar.org/chronicle/411/sativex.shtml. Retrieved on 2006-03-25.

117. Greenberg, Gary (2005-11-01). "Respectable Reefer". Mother Jones. http://www.motherjones.com/news/feature/2005/11/Respectable_Reefer-3.html. Retrieved on 2007-04-03.

118. Cosmos Online - Cannabis-like drug dims pain without high <http://www.cosmosmagazine.com/news/2366/cannabis-drug-dims-pain-without-high>

119. "Nabilone marijuana-based drug reduces fibromyalgia pain". www.news-medical.net. http://www.news-medical.net/?id=35301. Retrieved on 2008-05-31.

120. "Compare Marinol Prices on PharmacyChecker.com". www.pharmacychecker.com. http://www.pharmacychecker.com/Pricing.asp?DrugName=Marinol&DrugId=25680&DrugStrengthId=43149. Retrieved on 2008-05-31.

121. (cadth-acmts.ca)

122. "Marijuana - The First Twelve Thousand Years - 1. Cannabis in the Ancient World". www.druglibrary.org. http://www.druglibrary.org/schaffer/hemp/history/first12000/1.htm. Retrieved on 2008-06-06.

123. "History of Cannabis". BBC News. http://news.bbc.co.uk/1/hi/programmes/panorama/1632726.stm.

124. de Crespigny, Rafe. (2007). A Biographical Dictionary of Later Han to the Three Kingdoms (23-220 AD). Leiden: Koninklijke Brill. ISBN 9004156054. Page 332.

125. Wong, Ming (1976). La Médecine chinoise par les plantes. Le Corps a Vivre series. Éditions Tchou.

126. "The Ebers Papyrus The Oldest (confirmed) Written Prescriptions For Medical Marihuana era 1,550 BC". www.onlinepot.org. http://www.onlinepot.org/medical/eberspapyrus.htm. Retrieved on 2008-06-10.

127. "History of Cannabis". www.reefermadnessmuseum.org. http://www.reefermadnessmuseum.org/history/AEgyptian.htm. Retrieved on 2008-07-09.

128. Pain, Stephanie (2007-12-15). "The Pharaoh's pharmacists". New Scientist (Reed Business Information Ltd.). http://www.newscientist.com/channel/health/mg19626341.600-the-pharaohs-pharmacists.html.

129. Lise Manniche, An Ancient Egyptian Herbal, University of Texas Press, 1989, ISBN 978-0292704152

130. Unknown (2003-10-21). "The Religious and Medicinal Uses of Cannabis in China, India and Tibet". 66.102.1.104. http://66.102.1.104/scholar?hl=en&lr=&q=cache:ISqaTTCsRWsJ:vajrayana.faithweb.com/Touw.pdf+marijuana,+medicinal. Retrieved on 2009-04-26.

131. "The Haworth Press Online Catalog: Article Abstract". www.haworthpress.com. http://www.haworthpress.com/store/ArticleAbstract.asp?sid=0JN5HC HTFHLA9LA1NQVRUKQM7C3RB5A4&ID=4344. Retrieved on 2009-01-18.

132. Lozano, Indalecio (2001). "The Therapeutic Use of Cannabis sativa (L.) in Arabic Medicine". Journal of Cannabis Therapeutics 1 (1): 63–70. doi:10.1300/J175v01n01_05.

133. Mack, Allyson; Janet Elizabeth Joy (2001). Marijuana as Medicine?: The Science Beyond the Controversy. National Academy Press.

134. "Marijuana - The First Twelve Thousand Years - Reefer Racism". Druglibrary.org. http://www.druglibrary.org/schaffer/hemp/history/first12000/11.htm. Retrieved on 2009-04-26.

135. "Golden Guide". www.zauberpilz.com. http://www.zauberpilz.com/golden/g31-40.htm.

136. Zimmerman, Bill; Nancy Crumpacker and Rick Bayer (1998). Is Marijuana the Right Medicine for You?: A Factual Guide to Medical Uses of Marijuana. Keats Publishing. ISBN 0879839066.

137. "Cannabis: Effects". Lycos Retriever. Lycos, Inc.. http://www.lycos.com/info/cannabis--effects.html.

138. "Synthetic THC / Marinol". The Alliance for Reform of Drug Policy in Arkansas, Inc.. http://www.ardpark.org/marinol_research.htm.

139. "How does the cost of marijuana compare to the cost of Marinol?". Medical Marijuana ProCon.org. ProCon.org. http://medicalmarijuana.procon.org/viewanswers.asp?questionID=91.

140. McPartland, John M.; Russo, Ethan B.. "Cannabis and Cannabis Extracts: Greater Than the Sum of Their Parts?". Journal of Cannabis Therapeutics. International Association for Cannabis as Medicine. http://www.cannabis-med.org/membersonly/mo.php?aid=&fid=&mode=a&sid=.

141. Mack,Alison ; Joy, Janet (2001). Marijuana As Medicine. National Academy Press.

142. Russo, Ethan; Mathre, Mary Lynn; Byrne, Al; Velin, Robert; Bach, Paul J.; Sanchez-Ramos, Juan; Kirlin, Kristin A (2002). "Chronic Cannabis Use in the Compassionate Investigational New Drug Program: An Examination of Benefits and Adverse Effects of Legal Clinical Cannabis" (PDF). Journal of Cannabis Therapeutics (The Haworth Press, Inc.) 2 (1). http://www.medicalcannabis.com/PDF/Chronic_Cannabis.pdf.

143. US Govt. Patent Office. http://www.uspto.gov/

**144.** Physicians Are Not Bootleggers, The Bulletin of the History of Medicine, Summer 2008.

**145.** "The American College of Physicians Position Paper" (PDF). The American College of Physicians. 2008. http://www.acponline.org/advocacy/where_we_stand/other_issues/medmarijuana.pdf. Retrieved on 2008-02-20.

**146.** "Inter-Agency Advisory Regarding Claims That Smoked Marijuana Is a Medicine". Fda.gov. 2006-04-20. http://www.fda.gov/bbs/topics/NEWS/2006/NEW01362.html. Retrieved on 2009-04-26.

**147.** [4]^[dead link]

**148.** http://www.nationalmssociety.org/Sourcebook-Marijuana.asp

**149.** [5]^[dead link]

**150.** "ACS :: Smoking Marijuana May Increase Cancer Risk". Cancer.org. http://www.cancer.org/docroot/NWS/content/NWS_1_1x_Smoking_Marijuana_May_Increase_Cancer_Risk.asp. Retrieved on 2009-04-26.

**151.** "Cannabis and Medicine: Assessing the Science Base", Institute of Medicine, 1999.

**152.** Cannabis Appetite Boost Lacking in Cancer Study" The New York Times, May 13, 2001.

**153.** *Cannabis Vaporizer Combines Efficient Delivery of THC with Effective Suppression of Pyrolytic Compounds* By D. Gieringer *et al.* Journal of Cannabis Therapeutics, Vol. 4(1) 2004, [6]

**154.** *Evaluation of a Vaporizing Device (Volcano) for the Pulmonary Administration of Tetrahydrocannabinol.* By A. HAZEKAMP, R. RUHAAK, *et al.* JOURNAL OF PHARMACEUTICAL SCIENCES, VOL. 95, NO. 6, JUNE 2006 abstract

**155.** "Microbiological contaminants of marijuana". Hempfood.com. http://www.hempfood.com/IHA/iha01205.html. Retrieved on 2009-04-26.

**156.** "AFP: Austria allows cannabis for medical purposes". afp.google.com. http://afp.google.com/article/ALeqM5gMXaMnzKEu6FxfDVlCHd4xMcmEbg. Retrieved on 2008-07-21.

**157.** (French) Foire aux questions au sujet de la marihuana à des fins médicales, sur le site de Santé Canada

**158.** (English) « More pot, please: Demand booming for Prairie Plant's marijuana », CBC, 23 octobre 2006.

**159.** (English) A Review of the Cannabis Cultivation Contract between Health Canada and Prairie Plant Systems

**160.** (English) Court challenge aims to legalize all cannabis use

**161.** "The DEA Position On Marijuana". Usdoj.gov. http://www.usdoj.gov/dea/marijuana_position.html#smoked. Retrieved on 2009-04-26.

**162.** "Inter-Agency Advisory Regarding Claims That Smoked Marijuana Is a Medicine". Fda.gov. 2006-04-20. http://www.fda.gov/bbs/topics/news/2006/new01362.html. Retrieved on 2009-04-26.

**163.** "Opinion: US Government Holds Patent For Medical Marijuana, Shows Hipocrisy - Digital Journal: Your News Network". Digital Journal. 2008-07-07. http://www.digitaljournal.com/article/257008. Retrieved on 2009-04-26.

**164.** "In Memory: Robert Randall, Father of the Medical Marijuana Movement". 2001. http://www.november.org/razorwire/rzold/25/page35.html. Retrieved on 2008-02-21.

**165.** Debra J. Saunders (2009-01-29). "Two things Obama could do on medical marijuana". Sfgate.com. http://www.sfgate.com/cgi-bin/article.cgi?f=/c/a/2009/01/28/EDL415IA6F.DTL. Retrieved on 2009-04-26.

**166.** "Ron Paul". *Medical Marijuana Pro Con*. MPP.ORG. http://medicalmarijuana.procon.org/viewsource.asp?ID=1560.

**167.** http://ca.news.finance.yahoo.com/s/09072009/34/biz-f-business-wire-csi-appoints-dr-robert-melamede-ph-d-former.html

**168.** "In Pot We Trust (2007) (TV)". *The Internet Movie Database*. IMDb.com, Inc.. http://imdb.com/title/tt1069233/.

**169.** "William J. Bennett". *Biography of William J. Bennett*. Medical Marijuana ProCon.org. 2007-10-28. http://medicalmarijuana.procon.org/viewsource.asp?ID=1336. Retrieved on 2007-10-28.

**170.** Medical Marijuana: A Dream Up In Smoke? - Human Rights Magazine Fall 1997

**171.** Opposition set to snuff out medical marijuana bill | Daily Record, The (Baltimore) | Find Articles at BNET.com

**172.** "Romney Confronted". *CNN Video - Breaking News* (CNN). 2007-10-08. http://www.cnn.com/video/#/video/politics/2007/10/07/romney.confronted.cnn. Retrieved on 2007-10-08.

**173.** SignOnSanDiego.com > News > Politics - Medical marijuana remains in legal limbo

**174.** "Asa Hutchinson". *Biography of Asa Hutchinson*. Medical Marijuana ProCon.org. 2007-10-28. http://medicalmarijuana.procon.org/viewsource.asp?ID=1095. Retrieved on 2007-10-28.

**175.** "Richard Carmona". *Biography of Richard Carmona*. Medical Marijuana ProCon.org. 2007-10-28. http://medicalmarijuana.procon.org/viewsource.asp?ID=360. Retrieved on 2007-10-28.

**176.** "Candidates Positions on Medical Marijuana". Granitestaters.com. http://granitestaters.com/candidates/. Retrieved on 2009-04-26.

177. "Rush Limbaugh". *Biography of Rush Limbaugh*. Medical Marijuana ProCon. org. 2007-10-28. http://medicalmarijuana.procon.org/viewsource. asp?ID=5410. Retrieved on 2007-10-28.

# REFERENCES – CANNABIS IN THE UNITED STATES

1. http://www.fresnobee.com/local/story/1553061.html

2. The Editors; Roger Roffman, Wayne Hall, Mark A.R. Kleiman, Peter Reuter, Norm Stamper (2009-07-19). "If Marijuana Is Legal, Will Addiction Rise?". *The New York Times* (The New York Times Company). http://roomfordebate.blogs.nytimes.com/2009/07/19/if-marijuana-is-legal-will-addiction-rise/. Retrieved on 2009-07-27.

3. Degenhardt L, Chiu W-T, Sampson N, Kessler RC, Anthony JC, *et al.* 2008 Toward a Global View of Alcohol, Tobacco, Cannabis, and Cocaine Use: Findings from the WHO World Mental Health Surveys. PLoS Med 5(7): e141. doi:10.1371/journal.pmed.0050141

4. "2007 National Survey on Drug Use & Health: National Results: Appendix G: Selected Prevalence Tables". U.S. Department of Human Health and Services. 2007. http://oas.samhsa.gov/nsduh/2k7nsduh/AppG.htm#TabG-1. Retrieved on 2009-07-27.

5. Drug Approval Application Process

6. Meyer, Robert J. "Testimony before the Subcommittee on Criminal Justice, Drug Policy, and Human Resources, Committee on Government Reform". U.S. Food and Drug Administration. http://www.fda.gov/ola/2004/marijuana0401.html. Retrieved on 2007-09-15.

7. Inter-Agency Advisory Regarding Claims That Smoked Marijuana Is a Medicine

8. Pot activist's death probed - The Denver Post

9. "History of Marijuana". *Narconon International*. Association of Better Living and Education International. http://www.narconon.org/drug_information/marijuana_hist. Retrieved on 2008-02-12.

10. "In The Matter Of Marihuana Rescheduling Petition, Docket No. 86-22, Opinion and Recommended Ruling, Findings of Fact, Conclusions of Law and Decision of Administrative Law Judge Francis L. Young". *United States Department of Justice, Drug Enforcement Administration.* Carl E. Olsen. 1998-09-06. http://www.druglibrary.org/olsen/MEDICAL/YOUNG/young.html.

11. "Testimony by Robert J. Meyer, M.D., Director, Office of Drug Evaluation II, Center for Drug Evaluation and Research, Food and Drug Administration, U.S. Department of Health and Human Services before the Subcommittee on Criminal Justice, Drug Policy, and Human Resources, Committee on Government Reform, House of Representatives". United States Food and Drug Administration, Office of Legislation. http://www.fda.gov/ola/2004/marijuana0401.html.

12. "State Medical Marijuana Laws". *Medical Marijuana ProCon.org*. ProCon.org. http://medicalmarijuana.procon.org/viewresource.asp?resourceID=881.

13. "Active State Medical Marijuana Programs - NORML". norml.com. http://norml.com/index.cfm?Group_ID=3391. Retrieved on 2008-06-04.

14. "California Medical Marijuana Program". www.dhs.ca.gov. http://www.dhs.ca.gov/MMP/. Retrieved on 2008-05-30.

15. "California Attorney General Opinion on SB420" (PDF). ag.ca.gov. http://ag.ca.gov/opinions/pdfs/04-709.pdf. Retrieved on 2008-06-10.

16. "State by State Laws". http://norml.org. Retrieved on 2008-05-07.

17. http://www.stltoday.com/stltoday/news/stories.nsf/politics/story/CF5B266CF4358F0B862575CC0001E50E?OpenDocument

18. Cook, T; Powell D; Bradley T (2008-11-05). "California Passes Gay Marriage Ban, Legal Challenges to Come". ABC News. http://abcnews.go.com/TheLaw/Vote2008/Story?id=6184848&page=3. Retrieved on 2008-11-12.

19. http://www.nj.com/news/index.ssf/2009/06/new_jersey_wrestles_with_medic.html

20. "State of Oregon: Oregon Medical Marijuana Program (OMMP)". www.oregon.gov. http://www.oregon.gov/DHS/ph/ommp/. Retrieved on 2008-05-30.

21. "Oregon Medical Marijuana Program Data". oregon.gov. http://oregon.gov/DHS/ph/ommp/data.shtml. Retrieved on 2008-06-02.

22. Oregon Medical Marijuana Program (OMMP): Statistics

23. http://blogs.wsj.com/health/2009/06/17/rhode-island-joins-states-legalizing-sale-of-medical-marijuana/

24. "Chapter 69.51A RCW: Medical marijuana". apps.leg.wa.gov. http://apps.leg.wa.gov/RCW/default.aspx?cite=69.51A&full=true. Retrieved on 2008-06-02.

25. Patrick O'Driscoll (2005-11-03). "Denver votes to legalize marijuana possession". USA Today. http://www.usatoday.com/news/nation/2005-11-03-pot_x.htm. Retrieved on 2006-03-11.

26. http://www.boston.com/news/local/breaking_news/2008/11/question_2_setu.html

27. http://citizensbriefingbook.change.gov/ideas/ideaList.apexp?c=09a800000004fo6&lsi=2 - Retrieved 20 January 2009

28. http://www.fbi.gov/ucr/05cius/arrests/index.html FBI Uniform Crimes Report

29. http://drugwarfacts.org/cms/?q=node/53

30. http://www.whitehousedrugpolicy.gov/publications/marijuana_myths_facts/myth10.pdf

31. http://norml.org/index.cfm?Group_ID=7698

# GNU FREE DOCUMENTATION LICENSE

## 0. PREAMBLE

The purpose of this License is to make a manual, textbook, or other functional and useful document "free" in the sense of freedom: to assure everyone the effective freedom to copy and redistribute it, with or without modifying it, either commercially or noncommercially. Secondarily, this License preserves for the author and publisher a way to get credit for their work, while not being considered responsible for modifications made by others.

This License is a kind of "copyleft", which means that derivative works of the document must themselves be free in the same sense. It complements the GNU General Public License, which is a copyleft license designed for free software.

We have designed this License in order to use it for manuals for free software, because free software needs free documentation: a free program should come with manuals providing the same freedoms that the software does. But this License is not limited to software manuals; it can be used for any textual work, regardless of subject matter or whether it is published as a printed book. We recommend this License principally for works whose purpose is instruction or reference.

## 1. APPLICABILITY AND DEFINITIONS

This License applies to any manual or other work, in any medium, that contains a notice placed by the copyright holder saying it can be distributed under the terms of this License. Such a notice grants a world-wide, royalty-free license, unlimited in duration, to use that work under the conditions stated herein. The "Document", herein, refers to any such manual or work. Any member of the public is a licensee, and is addressed as "you". You accept the license if you copy, modify or distribute the work in a way requiring permission under copyright law.

A "Modified Version" of the Document means any work containing the Document or a portion of it, either copied verbatim, or with modifications and/or translated into another language.

A "Secondary Section" is a named appendix or a front-matter section of the Document that deals exclusively with the relationship of the publishers or authors of the Document to the Document's overall subject (or to related matters) and contains nothing that could fall directly within that overall subject. (Thus, if the Document is in part a textbook of mathematics, a Secondary Section may not explain any mathematics.) The relationship could be a matter of historical connection with the subject or with related matters, or of legal, commercial, philosophical, ethical or political position regarding them.

The "Invariant Sections" are certain Secondary Sections whose titles are designated, as being those of Invariant Sections, in the notice that says that the Document is released under this License. If a section does not fit the above definition of Secondary then it is not allowed to be designated as Invariant. The Document may contain zero Invariant Sections. If the Document does not identify any Invariant Sections then there are none.

The "Cover Texts" are certain short passages of text that are listed, as Front-Cover Texts or Back-Cover Texts, in the notice that says that the Document is released under this License. A Front-Cover Text may be at most 5 words, and a Back-Cover Text may be at most 25 words.

A "Transparent" copy of the Document means a machine-readable copy, represented in a format whose specification is available to the general public, that is suitable for revising the document straightforwardly with generic text editors or (for images composed of pixels) generic paint programs or (for drawings) some widely available drawing editor, and that is suitable for input to text formatters or for automatic translation to a variety of formats suitable for input to text formatters. A copy made in an otherwise Transparent file format whose markup, or absence of markup, has been arranged to thwart or discourage subsequent modification by readers is not Transparent. An image format is not Transparent if used for any substantial amount of text. A copy that is not "Transparent" is called "Opaque".

Examples of suitable formats for Transparent copies include plain ASCII without markup, Texinfo input format, LaTeX input format, SGML or XML using a publicly available DTD, and standard-conforming simple HTML, PostScript or PDF designed for human modification. Examples of transparent image formats include PNG, XCF and JPG. Opaque formats include proprietary formats that can be read and edited only by proprietary word processors, SGML or XML for which the DTD and/or processing tools are not generally available, and the machine-generated HTML, PostScript or PDF produced by some word processors for output purposes only.

The "Title Page" means, for a printed book, the title page itself, plus such following pages as are needed to hold, legibly, the material this License requires to appear in the title page. For works in formats which do not have any title page as such, "Title Page" means the text near the most prominent appearance of the work's title, preceding the beginning of the body of the text.

A section "Entitled XYZ" means a named subunit of the Document whose title either is precisely XYZ or contains XYZ in parentheses following text that translates XYZ in another language. (Here XYZ stands for a specific section name mentioned below, such as "Acknowledgements", "Dedications", "Endorsements", or "History".) To "Preserve the Title" of such a section when you modify the Document means that it remains a section "Entitled XYZ" according to this definition.

The Document may include Warranty Disclaimers next to the notice which states that this License applies to the Document. These Warranty Disclaimers are considered to be included by reference in this License, but only as regards disclaiming warranties: any other implication that these Warranty Disclaimers may have is void and has no effect on the meaning of this License.

## 2. VERBATIM COPYING

You may copy and distribute the Document in any medium, either commercially or noncommercially, provided that this License, the copyright notices, and the license notice saying this License applies to the Document are reproduced in all copies, and that you add no other conditions whatsoever to those of this License. You may not use technical measures to obstruct or control the reading or further copying of the copies you make or distribute. However, you may accept compensation in exchange for copies. If you distribute a large enough number of copies you must also follow the conditions in section 3.

You may also lend copies, under the same conditions stated above, and you may publicly display copies.

## 3. COPYING IN QUANTITY

If you publish printed copies (or copies in media that commonly have printed covers) of the Document, numbering more than 100, and the Document's license notice requires Cover Texts, you must enclose the copies in covers that carry, clearly and legibly, all these Cover Texts: Front-Cover Texts on the front cover, and Back-Cover Texts on the back cover. Both covers must also clearly and legibly identify you as the publisher of these copies. The front cover must present the full title with all words of the title equally prominent and visible. You may add other material on the covers in addition. Copying with changes limited to the covers, as long as they preserve the title of the Document and satisfy these conditions, can be treated as verbatim copying in other respects.

If the required texts for either cover are too voluminous to fit legibly, you should put the first ones listed (as many as fit reasonably) on the actual cover, and continue the rest onto adjacent pages.

If you publish or distribute Opaque copies of the Document numbering more than 100, you must either include a machine-readable Transparent copy along with each Opaque copy, or state in or with each Opaque copy a computer-network location from which the general network-using public has access to download using public-standard network protocols a complete Transparent copy of the Document, free of added material. If you use the latter option, you must take reasonably prudent steps, when you begin distribution of Opaque copies in quantity, to ensure that this Transparent copy will remain thus accessible at the stated location until at least one year after the last time you distribute an Opaque copy (directly or through your agents or retailers) of that edition to the public.

It is requested, but not required, that you contact the authors of the Document well before redistributing any large number of copies, to give them a chance to provide you with an updated version of the Document.

## 4. MODIFICATIONS

You may copy and distribute a Modified Version of the Document under the conditions of sections 2 and 3 above, provided that you release the Modified Version under precisely this License, with the Modified Version filling the role of the Document, thus licensing distribution and modification of the Modified Version to whoever possesses a copy of it. In addition, you must do these things in the Modified Version:

**A.** Use in the Title Page (and on the covers, if any) a title distinct from that of the Document, and from those of previous versions (which should, if there were any, be listed in the History section of the Document). You may use the same title as a previous version if the original publisher of that version gives permission.

**B.** List on the Title Page, as authors, one or more persons or entities responsible for authorship of the modifications in the Modified Version, together with at least five of the principal authors of the Document (all of its principal authors, if it has fewer than five), unless they release you from this requirement.

**C.** State on the Title page the name of the publisher of the Modified Version, as the publisher.

**D.** Preserve all the copyright notices of the Document.

**E.** Add an appropriate copyright notice for your modifications adjacent to the other copyright notices.

**F.** Include, immediately after the copyright notices, a license notice giving the public permission to use the Modified Version under the terms of this License, in the form shown in the Addendum below.

**G.** Preserve in that license notice the full lists of Invariant Sections and required Cover Texts given in the Document's license notice.

**H.** Include an unaltered copy of this License.

**I.** Preserve the section Entitled "History", Preserve its Title, and add to it an item stating at least the title, year, new authors, and publisher of the Modified Version as given on the Title Page. If there is no section Entitled "History" in the Document, create one stating the title, year, authors, and publisher of the Document as given on its Title Page, then add an item describing the Modified Version as stated in the previous sentence.

**J.** Preserve the network location, if any, given in the Document for public access to a Transparent copy of the Document, and likewise the network locations given in the Document for previous versions it was based on. These may be placed in the "History" section. You may omit a network location for a work that was published at least four years before the Document itself, or if the original publisher of the version it refers to gives permission.

**K.** For any section entitled "Acknowledgements" or "Dedications", Preserve the Title of the section, and preserve in the section all the substance and tone of each of the contributor acknowledgements and/or dedications given therein.

**L.** Preserve all the Invariant Sections of the Document, unaltered in their text and in their titles. Section numbers or the equivalent are not considered part of the section titles.

**M.** Delete any section entitled "Endorsements". Such a section may not be included in the Modified Version.

**N.** Do not retitle any existing section to be entitled "Endorsements" or to conflict in title with any Invariant Section.

**O.** Preserve any Warranty Disclaimers.

If the Modified Version includes new front-matter sections or appendices that qualify as Secondary Sections and contain no material copied from the Document, you may at your option designate some or all of these sections as Invariant. To do this, add their titles to the list of Invariant Sections in the Modified Version's license notice. These titles must be distinct from any other section titles.

You may add a section entitled "Endorsements", provided it contains nothing but endorsements of your Modified Version by various parties—for example, statements of peer review or that the text has been approved by an organization as the authoritative definition of a standard.

You may add a passage of up to five words as a Front-Cover Text, and a passage of up to 25 words as a Back-Cover Text, to the end of the list of Cover Texts in the Modified Version. Only one passage of Front-Cover Text and one of Back-Cover Text may be added by (or through arrangements made by) any one entity. If the Document already includes a Cover Text for the same cover, previously added by you or by arrangement made by the same entity you are acting on behalf of, you may not add another; but you may replace the old one, on explicit permission from the previous publisher that added the old one.

The author(s) and publisher(s) of the Document do not by this License give permission to use their names for publicity for or to assert or imply endorsement of any Modified Version.

## 5. COMBINING DOCUMENTS

You may combine the Document with other documents released under this License, under the terms defined in section 4 above for modified versions, provided that you include in the combination all of the Invariant Sections of all of the original documents, unmodified, and list them all as Invariant Sections of your combined work in its license notice, and that you preserve all their Warranty Disclaimers.

The combined work need only contain one copy of this License, and multiple identical Invariant Sections may be replaced with a single copy. If there are multiple Invariant Sections with the same name but different contents, make the title of each such section unique by adding at the end of it, in parentheses, the name of the original author or publisher of that section if known, or else a unique number. Make the same adjustment to the section titles in the list of Invariant Sections in the license notice of the combined work.

In the combination, you must combine any sections entitled "History" in the various original documents, forming one section entitled "History";

likewise combine any sections entitled "Acknowledgements", and any sections entitled "Dedications". You must delete all sections entitled "Endorsements."

## 6. COLLECTIONS OF DOCUMENTS

You may make a collection consisting of the Document and other documents released under this License, and replace the individual copies of this License in the various documents with a single copy that is included in the collection, provided that you follow the rules of this License for verbatim copying of each of the documents in all other respects.

You may extract a single document from such a collection, and distribute it individually under this License, provided you insert a copy of this License into the extracted document, and follow this License in all other respects regarding verbatim copying of that document.

## 7. AGGREGATION WITH INDEPENDENT WORKS

A compilation of the Document or its derivatives with other separate and independent documents or works, in or on a volume of a storage or distribution medium, is called an "aggregate" if the copyright resulting from the compilation is not used to limit the legal rights of the compilation's users beyond what the individual works permit. When the Document is included in an aggregate, this License does not apply to the other works in the aggregate which are not themselves derivative works of the Document.

If the Cover Text requirement of section 3 is applicable to these copies of the Document, then if the Document is less than one half of the entire aggregate, the Document's Cover Texts may be placed on covers that bracket the Document within the aggregate, or the electronic equivalent of covers if the Document is in electronic form. Otherwise they must appear on printed covers that bracket the whole aggregate.

## 8. TRANSLATION

Translation is considered a kind of modification, so you may distribute translations of the Document under the terms of section 4. Replacing Invariant Sections with translations requires special permission from their copyright holders, but you may include translations of some or all Invariant Sections in addition to the original versions of these Invariant Sections. You may include a translation of this License, and all the license notices in the Document, and any Warranty Disclaimers, provided that you also include the original English version of this License and the original versions of those notices and disclaimers. In case of a disagreement between the translation and the original version of this License or a notice or disclaimer, the original version will prevail.

If a section in the Document is entitled "Acknowledgements", "Dedications", or "History", the requirement (section 4) to Preserve its Title (section 1) will typically require changing the actual title.

## 9. TERMINATION

You may not copy, modify, sublicense, or distribute the Document except as expressly provided for under this License. Any other attempt to copy, modify, sublicense or distribute the Document is void, and will automatically terminate your rights under this License. However, parties who have received copies, or rights, from you under this License will not have their licenses terminated so long as such parties remain in full compliance.

## 10. FUTURE REVISIONS OF THIS LICENSE

The Free Software Foundation may publish new, revised versions of the GNU Free Documentation License from time to time. Such new versions will be similar in spirit to the present version, but may differ in detail to address new problems or concerns. See http://www.gnu.org/copyleft/.

Each version of the License is given a distinguishing version number. If the Document specifies that a particular numbered version of this License "or any later version" applies to it, you have the option of following the terms and conditions either of that specified version or of any later version that has been published (not as a draft) by the Free Software Foundation. If the Document does not specify a version number of this License, you may choose any version ever published (not as a draft) by the Free Software Foundation.

# INDEX